The Unwanted Undead Adventurer [4] Yu Okano / Illustrator: Jaian

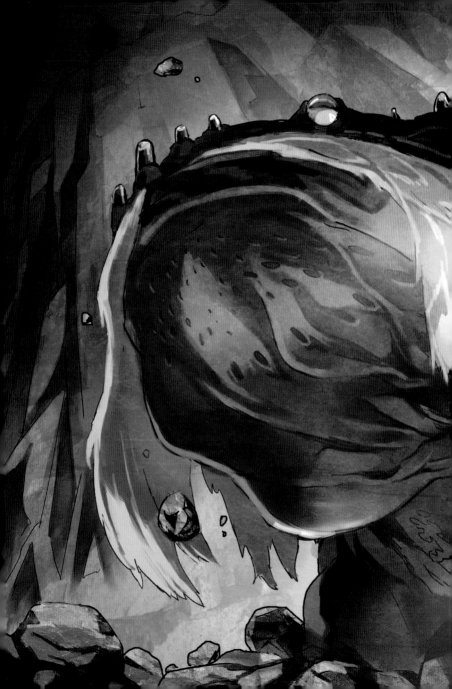

...an earth dragon.

[fourth / 4] The Unwanted Undead Adventurer

Yu Okano
Illustrator: Jaian

Clope

Proprietor of the Three-Pronged Harpoon. Produces special weapons and armor that match Rentt's requirements.

Isabel Cariello

Loris's wife. Runs the Red Wyvern Pavilion with him. Business is good.

Loris Cariello

Proprietor of the Red Wyvern Pavilion, a tavern and eatery. Because he was saved by Rentt in the labyrinth, Rentt dines in his tavern for free.

Myullias Raiza

A Saint of the Church of Lobelia. Blessed by the spirits, she is capable of channeling divinity. Wields the powers of healing and purification.

Nive Maris

A Gold-class adventurer, as well as a vampire hunter. She is seen by many as the closest individual to Platinum-class.

Luka

Clope's Wife. Assists him in the daily operations of the Three-Pronged Harpoon.

Story

The Thousand-Year Bronze-class adventurer, Rentt, finds himself becoming an undead after being consumed by a mythical dragon. Evolving into a thrall, he manages to sneak back into the town with the aid of Rina Rupaage, a budding adventurer. Now hiding out in Lorraine's abode, he changes his name before once again setting off on the path of becoming a Mithril-class adventurer. Now having evolved into a lesser vampire, Rentt sets off to the New Moon Dungeon in search of materials, all for the sake of crafting a weapon for his disciple, Alize.

Meanwhile, a Saint from the Church of Lobelia and a Gold-class vampire hunter find themselves visiting Maalt around the same time...

Characters

Sheila Ibarss

Receptionist at the adventurer's guild. Knows Rentt's secret.

Lorraine Vivie

Scholar and Silver-class adventurer. Has been offering her support to Rentt ever since he became an undead.

Rentt Faina

An adventurer aspiring to reach Mithril-class. Became an undead after he was consumed by a dragon in the labyrinth.

Edel

A monster commonly referred to as a puchi suri. Became Rentt's familiar after sucking his blood in the basement of Maalt's Second Orphanage.

Alize

A young girl living at the orphanage. Dreams of becoming an adventurer. Currently Lorraine and Rentt's disciple.

Rina Rupaage

A new adventurer who helped Rentt sneak into Maalt after he had evolved into a ghoul.

Idoles Rogue

A knight belonging to the First Brigade of the Kingdom of Yaaran. Has a younger sister by the name of Rina.

Isaac Hart

A servant of the Latuule family. Is capable enough to take on the Tarasque Swamp on his own.

Laura Latuule

The current head of the Latuule family. Loves collecting magical items of all kinds. Rentt is contracted to periodically deliver Dragon Blood Blossoms to her from the swamp.

THE UNWANTED UNDEAD ADVENTURER: VOLUME 4
By Yu Okano

Translated by Shirley Yeung & Noah Rozenberg
Edited by CHaSE & Suzanne Seals
English Print Cover by Mitach

First published in Japan in 2018 by OVERLAP Inc., Tokyo.
Publication rights for this English edition arranged through OVERLAP Inc., Tokyo.

Find more books like this one at www.j-novel.club!

Managing Director: Samuel Pinansky
Light Novel Line Manager: Chi Tran
Managing Editor: Jan Mitsuko Cash
Managing Translator: Kristi Fernandez
QA Manager: Hannah N. Carter
Marketing Manager: Stephanie Hii

ISBN: 978-1-7183-5743-3
Printed in Korea
First Printing: February 2022
10 9 8 7 6 5 4 3 2 1

[C O N T E N T S]

 Chapter 1:   To the New Moon Dungeon

I found myself with some free time on my hands. I'd been summoned by the adventurer's guild earlier today, so I assumed it was about the payout from the tarasque carcass. With that incoming money in mind, I made plans to visit the blacksmith, armorer, and even a general merchant. I even ensured that I had enough time to complete my tasks. However, while I'd obtained quite a bit of coin from the sale of the tarasque, the amount I received was hardly enough for the extravagant schedule I'd initially planned for today.

Ah, yes. A failure on my part...

While the trips to the blacksmith and general merchant were to procure basic adventuring equipment and weapons for Alize, the trip to the armorer was personal in nature. Of course, I had a fair amount of clothing I'd accumulated over my lifetime spent as Rentt Faina, a regular human. But those hardly had any openings in the back. As such, it was safe to assume my wings would have a hard time finding their way out of said garments—and that was a bit of an understatement.

It was with those thoughts in mind that I set out to purchase some custom clothing. It was all made to order, and it was specifically tailored to brave the dangers of the dungeons. As a result, it was considerably more expensive. I'd expected that the payout from the tarasque would be more than enough, but, of course, I was very much mistaken.

Damn it.

To make matters worse, the clothing I originally owned was already quite tattered and in dire need of repairs. Due to my relatively low income at the start of my journey, I hardly made any unnecessary purchases. On top of that, I'd been wearing the clothes on me for quite a while now—through both my ghoul and thrall evolutions. They were dirty, to say the least, and they had unusual debris stuck in the fabric. After all, blood and fragments of flesh weren't exactly normal to find in clothing.

I did my laundry daily…but that wasn't the issue here. Now that I was almost indistinguishable from a normal human, the mere thought of me wearing the clothes I'd worn when I was still more monstrous… Well, it was a difficult thought. This was an opportunity as good as any other, so I set off to purchase replacements.

Unfortunately…it wasn't meant to be.

The main concern, of course, was of coin. I'd receive a fair sum from the dissection and sale of the carcasses, yes, but if I ordered some custom clothing, I'd hardly have anything left for Alize's weapons, equipment, and the like… Not to mention Lorraine's tutoring fees.

I suddenly felt myself under immense financial strain. I could feel the weight of debt crushing my very being.

Ah, to be an individual with multiple debts… To think I'd have to live like this, hand-to-mouth and shouldered with debt… What sins, exactly, had I committed in my past life to warrant this? I couldn't help but think I should have lived a more pious, upright life in my previous incarnation.

Well… In any case, I supposed this was how things were. Rather than complaining repeatedly that I had little in the way of coin, I should instead come up with some sort of plan. Yes, a plan to earn a *considerable* sum of coin. Sooner or later, the undamaged carapace of the tarasque would sell, and, when it did, I'd be blessed with a remarkable windfall. Until then, I'd just have to continue living my hand-to-mouth lifestyle, saving where I could...

But alas...

These thought patterns were precisely why I was currently in this unfortunate situation.

I shook my head. If I were to live my life depending on the next windfall to come, I'd never have any sizable amount of savings to call my own.

Rentt, are you not an individual who is capable of restraint? You did save up enough coin to purchase a magic bag before. If you put your mind to it, saving some coin is hardly an impossible task. Surely there is some way I could set about solving this problem. Some...idea... Hmm. Think, Rentt... To save...to scrimp.

What was the most basic means by which an adventurer could save themselves some coin...?

Ah, yes—the provision of materials. An adventurer could present the craftsman with the appropriate ingredients when creating new equipment, gathered by their own hand.

At least, that was what I thought. However, due to the currently unique nature of my body, and the fact that the equipment I required was largely made to my specifications, gathering the appropriate materials was difficult at best.

Take my sword, for instance. An instrument capable of channeling mana, spirit, and divinity. Surely such a feat wouldn't be possible without some rare, hard-to-obtain materials. In addition, few craftsmen would be so eager to educate an adventurer specifically on how their equipment was made. This made things difficult, because I didn't even know what to bring the craftsmen in the first place.

I could place an order and be told by the establishment what I had to fetch; even so, unless I was explicitly instructed on what to bring, I couldn't just assume. See, only a skilled craftsman would know what they required to craft an item. This would make attempting to save on the construction of my weapons and equipment problematic.

But for Alize...

Yes, she could use a stronger weapon, or at least one that met my expectations in terms of quality. But there was no need for her very first weapon to be overly fancy. If an adventurer were to use a specially constructed weapon from the very start, they'd become dependent upon it, eventually leading to imbalances in their martial prowess. In fact, there was a high chance of said adventurer becoming one that was severely lacking in adaptability. While that wasn't strictly fatal for an adventurer, you should be prepared for all eventualities. For her sake, I should guide Alize away from this potential pitfall.

All things considered, gathering the materials for Alize's equipment by hand wasn't too bad an idea. Average materials with average performance... That's what I'd set out to gather. It was by no means an arduous task, and, thankfully, I had some free time on my hands. I could very well use the entire afternoon to scour the New Moon Dungeon.

Hmm... If the search took longer than expected, I'd likely return to Lorraine's abode tomorrow morning. I supposed I should make a trip back and let her know. Even if I had to work through the night, I'd just keep moving until I completely ran out of stamina. I had no need for sleep, after all. My stamina had become somewhat inexhaustible in nature, a fact I'd discovered having lived this way thus far. A special trait of the undead, you could say. Mental strain could possibly build up over time, but that would be the only sort of exhaustion I'd refer to if I spoke of it.

Now that I had an idea of what I wanted to do, I turned, intending to discuss matters with Lorraine back at her abode.

"A weapon for Alize? You do have to prepare one, yes… But is there really a need to assemble the very raw materials themselves?" was Lorraine's response as I informed her of my thoughts upon my return.

She was hardly disagreeing. If anything, she was expressing her thoughts on the matter. In fact, it wasn't hard to understand why she felt that way. In most cases, equipment for new adventurers was usually settled by blacksmiths and armorers; such equipment was hardly difficult to manufacture.

However…

"It's a matter of coin, Lorraine. I thought to save on costs and decided to gather the materials myself…"

"Ah, is that so? I understand then. In that case…you have yet to sell the tarasque carcass?" Lorraine inquired.

If anything, Lorraine had most likely already figured this out this very morning, and, as it turned out, it had gone just as she predicted. I continued my explanation, all the while feeling a little deflated at the accuracy of Lorraine's deductions.

"Yes… The matter became quite troublesome indeed…"

"Hmm? Explain yourself, Rentt."

I supposed even Lorraine hadn't envisioned the entire picture, given the strange turns in recent events. Lorraine remained inquisitive, her head tilted, as I explained what exactly occurred in the guild's dissection chamber. As I did, Lorraine's expression slowly changed to one of worry and exasperation.

"It would seem like sticking your head into strange affairs has become quite the regular occurrence for you…"

Quite exasperated.

"Don't be like that, Lorraine. For starters, it was the auctioneer who requested this of me. The corpse wouldn't sell itself if it were simply left there. It's also a large, somewhat respectable establishment, so ensuring our interests align would lead to rather…considerable gains in the long term. Don't you think so?"

"Yes, yes. I suppose there are merits to the whole thing, and it's not exactly a situation that can simply be ignored. However, consider this. The risk of your true identity being discovered is very real. In this particular case…that would be the sole, but still quite large, demerit."

I could hardly argue with the validity of her statements. However, so long as I continued living in Maalt, I'd eventually be forced to deal with either issue. When I thought about it that way, I somehow felt being bolder with the entire auction affair was the right way to go.

I expressed these thoughts to Lorraine.

"I do understand your angle, Rentt. Hmm… Personally, I would advise against it, but it is true those two problems present themselves as inevitable developments. If not here, then another place, another time… You would be equally as likely to get found out. If one were to think about it in that particular way…I suppose your idea wouldn't exactly be a bad choice."

It appeared Lorraine understood my line of reasoning. But she wasn't quite finished yet.

"If you sense any danger, any danger at all—escape as quickly as you can. It's not something I enjoy thinking about…but you see, even lesser vampires are worth quite a hefty sum. I wouldn't discount the existence of individuals who seek to capture them alive. If you headed into this whole thing with the aim of selling something at an auction, then woke up to find yourself as one of the items in the catalog… I cannot even laugh about this. If the time ever comes, I will assist you in escaping Maalt…escaping beyond the borders of Yaaran. So…do keep your wits about you, Rentt."

Lorraine's expression was grave. I nodded deeply in reply.

"I understand…"

However, something Lorraine said caught my attention.

"How much, exactly, could you sell a vampire for…?"

For a moment, Lorraine once again looked exasperated, perhaps because I seemed to show little concern for the dangers I could potentially be exposing myself to. But she soon gave it some thought and answered me seriously.

"Well… It would be raining platinum coins, Rentt. Not a colossal enough sum to swim in, I suppose, but surely not an amount an ordinary person could hope to pay…" Lorraine's brows furrowed, then she continued her train of thought. "You… Rentt, You don't mean to tell me… Are you attempting to sell yourself for funds?"

Lorraine's gaze bored into me as she narrowed her eyes.

"Don't be daft, Lorraine!" I shook my head in a panic. "There's no way I could do anything of the sort!"

Lorraine was quick to continue on. "No, Rentt, not in that fashion—at the very least, not your entire self… More along the lines of, say, blood or flesh samples. There is a possibility of you doing that, I suppose…"

I swallowed deeply. Lorraine was right—I had considered it…at some point. Just a tiny bit. I'd thought of the prospect only ever so slightly. Vampire blood had quite the medicinal value to nobles, you see. It was seen as an elixir of everlasting life, of immortality. While I wasn't sure how much of an effect said blood would have, I was sure to obtain a handsome amount of coin for it should I ever attempt to sell a vial at an auction. The auctioneer would certainly have some means of determining the blood's authenticity, so they'd be able to verify if it truly came from a monster. A vampire, to be precise. So long as one had enough coin, it was possible to send a sample straight to the Monster Research Institution at the capital of Yaaran. There, the sample could be adequately tested to verify its authenticity. As such, I'd thought it a fast and easy way to earn vast amounts of coin.

But I wasn't entirely reckless and had given the matter more careful thought. While the blood of vampires had the effect of bestowing immortality unto an individual, namely by turning them into an undead as well, it also had another purpose, its original purpose, perhaps: a vampire's blood was used to create underlings, familiars.

By that line of reasoning…would an individual who drank my blood become another one of my familiars? Much like Edel, the puchi suri, had.

Like…Edel though? That…would be most troubling. But I should set that thought aside. In any case, having an increase in the amount of familiars, just like that…

Logically, we could assume only the rich and powerful would be able to purchase something as expensive as vampire blood, or at least consciously desire it. It would certainly feel like a net gain to suddenly have an underling that had financial and social power, but I couldn't quite wrap my head around suddenly being able to command another individual in such a fashion. "Right, you work for me now," I'd say… No. It was no good. I couldn't picture myself with such a disposition.

No…more like impossible. That was the overall feeling I got.

In the end, I shook my head, as if these thoughts never crossed my mind.

"No, I never had such thoughts. I was just thinking about the dangers involved… Coin is an easy metric to understand. I was just… slightly taken in by the image."

Honestly speaking…the very thought of it raining platinum coins was quite terrifying in and of itself. Under no circumstances should I ever get caught.

Lorraine's monetary estimate, however, largely factored in the fact that I was a special case. By comparison, the more common lesser vampire would still fetch a good amount of coin, albeit a less ridiculous amount. They were seen more occasionally, despite being rare monsters, but they were also incredibly difficult to capture—that was the truth of it.

Most vampires tended to live in a cluster of sorts, commonly and collectively referred to as a "flock," with the highest-ranked vampire dominating all the rest. Ordinarily, it was a middle vampire acting as a de facto leader, dictating the actions of the lesser vampires under its command. In turn, thralls and human servants answered to lesser vampires. In such a case, even if you were to somehow capture a lesser vampire, there was still the influence of its leader, the middle vampire, to consider. For instance, its blood could be remotely controlled. It could be made to go berserk and then detonated by its leader, perhaps while the lesser vampire was being detained by its captors. After it was robbed of its powers by the middle vampire that created it in the first place, its vampiric strength would have nowhere to go, and the resultant forces would cause it to become unable to maintain its humanoid form. At least, that was one explanation for the phenomenon, with the real reason for this happening remaining unknown to this day.

The important takeaway from this was that lesser vampires could die the very moment they were captured, or perhaps shortly after they'd been captured. Their powers would be stripped from them by higher ranking vampires, then they'd explode. The flying pieces of flesh and bodily fluids would no longer have vampiric properties. This made it easy to understand the difficulty in capturing them. Really, it was more the futility of the affair even if you were to capture them.

But in my case...there'd be no high-ranking vampire to detonate me even if I were caught. Taking all this into consideration, even materials from a lesser vampire would be considerably rare and would fetch a high price. Excluding special cases like me, the only vampires that could be captured were solitary lesser vampires that naturally resided in the dungeons. With the exception of those individuals, most lesser vampires would have a leader and belong to a flock.

I now understood just how rare of an occurrence I was. I would surely be hunted and caught.

Terrifying...

Simply put, the vampire materials floating around these lands were either harvested from a leader or from lesser vampires that didn't have their powers stripped by their superiors upon capture. As for the vial I'd obtained from the Latuule family, I couldn't be absolutely certain. However, I hadn't felt any presence dominating my mind thus far, so I assumed it was been blood from the latter. Of course, there was always the possibility I was simply too far away, or that the powers within me were actively fighting this supposed domination... Whatever the case, so long as it remained dormant or under control, there wasn't much point in overly worrying about it.

Laura had warned me of the dangers involved, so if anything did happen... I supposed I'd have to cross that bridge when I came to it. And at that point in time, I had felt like I couldn't reach my next stage of Existential Evolution unless I drank the contents of the vial. In the end, I couldn't find any other solution or path forward, and regretting it after the fact would take me nowhere.

"Is that right...? Very well, then. In any case...do be careful, Rentt. Oh, yes, you were going to gather materials, right? If so, I have a few requests of my own. You may deduct the relevant expenses from your tuition fees."

Lorraine rattled off a list of items she wanted, including a few magical ores and various materials. It didn't take long to realize what her goals were, judging by the items she'd asked for.

"Are you thinking of gifting Alize something as well?"

"Verily so. If I am to teach her the ways of the mage...she will surely need a magic catalyst, if not several. I also intend to deliver some lectures on the creation of catalysts...hence the materials."

"I suppose that's why you asked for several of the same thing..."

My guess was ever so slightly off though. Magic in general benefits from the effects of a catalyst. This allows the mage to cast spells more easily and amplifies the magical output. In some cases, certain types of spells require a catalyst to be cast, and at those times a mage is expected to be capable of crafting their own catalyst. This was why mages generally had a basic grasp of alchemy. It was good to gain practical experience, which was probably why Lorraine wanted to educate Alize on this.

I was included in the lesson too, of course—materials for three people, after all. That much was clear.

"That is the gist of it, yes. One's first weapon is a special thing. I thought it would be good for Alize to try her hand at the subject."

Judging by how Lorraine described it, I could infer that creating one's first catalyst wasn't something a run-of-the-mill mage could do. A catalyst required a certain degree of technique and skill, so even a basic catalyst of average output was by no means a simple affair. For Lorraine to teach Alize how to go about it... I supposed it was also Lorraine's wish for her student to enjoy her lessons and training. I, too, wanted Alize to have some enjoyment.

"Are you not doing the same, Rentt?" Lorraine asked. "You claim to gather materials in the name of saving some coin, but is that really all there is to it? If you really just wanted something in your bag, a vial of blood here and there would be more than enough to do it. You, however, decided to gather materials by your own hand, all for the sake of creating a weapon—a gift for Alize. And so the two of us end up doing the exact same thing. How very peculiar..."

Peculiar? Was it really...? No, I didn't think so.

"Is that not something any master would do for their student? In fact, it is said that such were the traditions, a long time ago, that a student's first weapon would be a gift from their master."

Nowadays, it was more common for a student to procure their own weapon. It made perfect sense, considering the practice of taking students or disciples under one's wing was becoming increasingly uncommon. In addition, those who did have private tutors of some sort were often well-off.

"An old practice, yes." Lorraine nodded. "Few engage in the practice now...but I suppose there is no issue in us reviving the tradition."

Lorraine smiled at her own suggestion.

And so it came to be that I found myself arriving at the New Moon Dungeon. Of course, this was all for the sake of procuring materials to craft Alize's weapon.

Skeletons and slimes were a common sight on the first floor, and orcs were found on the second—such were the names of these compartmentalized areas. Since the dungeon's total amount of floors remained unknown, I wasn't sure what to call its deepest level. Whatever the case, it was quite a deep dungeon. By contrast, the Water Moon Dungeon seemingly ended on the very first floor... discounting the unknown areas and that one strange teleporter, but that was neither here nor there. To the general public's knowledge, that was the only known floor of the Water Moon Dungeon.

"My time in the spotlight... Who knows when or where..." I muttered to no one in particular.

In the past, I'd taken pains to walk long, circuitous paths around the first floor, all for the sake of filling out the Map of Akasha. Now, however, I found myself leisurely strolling through the halls. Although it was the most shallow floor of the dungeon, monsters did appear, as par for the course. You could savagely slay the monsters that showed themselves and impress upon this floor's denizens that they had no chance of winning. An adventurer walking calmly along, however, would most likely be assaulted one way or another, regardless of their innate strength.

I just found myself walking along without a care in the world, watching Edel fighting goblins and slimes right before my eyes. Since I planned to perform a thorough search of the dungeon today, I had brought Edel along to assist. His small size helped him easily locate and retrieve more minute materials in the area. Unexpectedly though, Edel chose to make himself useful in a combative capacity instead.

He wasn't exactly a huge boost to my combat potential... Regardless of his large size, he was still a puchi suri. The fighting capabilities of a puchi suri were lower than those of a goblin or slime; even a child of about ten years of age had a reasonable chance of defeating one as long as they had a weapon of some sort. Puchi suri were truly the absolute weakest type of monster. Even though there had been quite the show of strength during our encounter with the tarasque, my assumption was that that was the result of Edel snatching my reserves of power to strengthen himself. Basically, as long as I didn't provide him with mana, there would be a limit to his capabilities.

But reality was quite different. I was, at this point in time, consciously restricting the amount of power I shared with Edel. While he'd initially taken a noticeable chunk of my reserves without any indication, I discovered after the event that I was able to control and limit the flow of power from myself to my familiar. But regardless of that...I now bore witness to Edel taking on goblins and slimes alike without many issues.

Edel's small body…wasn't all that small any more. He was, say, about the size of an average goblin's head. He freely darted this way and that around the monsters, scaling the walls and launching himself at the them, body slamming them in the process.

As a Bronze-class adventurer, I had to infuse my single, well-placed attack with spirit to expose a slime's core. Slimes were troublesome buggers. Edel, on the other hand, began spinning during his body slams, using the resultant centrifugal force to disperse the slime's body into fine powder. The slime's fragments found themselves unable to reform and were now just stationary on the ground.

"…Gigi!" A goblin sputtered, as if bewildered by the sheer destructive power of Edel's body slam. Before it could react, however, Edel had already closed in, and the goblin found itself unable to avoid my familiar's attack. With a most intense, high-speed rotation, Edel's entire body slammed straight into the goblin's head, pulverizing it in the process. From my angle, it was almost as if the head had been blown apart by an explosive force.

It was a most grotesque sight…

"…Linpio."

With a wave of my hand as the incantation left my lips, a soft, glowing light enveloped Edel for a brief moment. As soon as it appeared, the light faded, leaving a pitch-black—well, he was pitch-black to begin with—clean Edel. No more spatterings of gore on his fur. As he was covered in goblin blood, guts, and bits of pulverized slime mere moments ago, it was only imperative I cleaned him.

Even so...cleansing him now may have been a bit of a wasted effort. We'd crossed paths with many monsters on our journey here, and we would unmistakably encounter some more as we ventured deeper. Edel would surely become filthy again soon enough.

I was hardly concerned about some streaks of blood and monster fragments, however. It was a given. I'd also swung my sword here and there and dissected the monsters we'd slain. Adventurers in the dungeons didn't really have high standards of hygiene.

But in Edel's case...the circumstances were once again slightly different. His basic form of attack was to tackle his foes while spinning at high speeds. The aim was to pulverize the enemy with his sheer speed and centrifugal force. From that, it was easy to conclude that Edel would quickly dirty himself in a similar fashion again. I supposed I would just have to cleanse him with Linpio each and every time then.

Linpio was a type of life magic I'd picked up recently. Offensive magic was one thing, but so long as you understood the theory, structure, and incantation of life magic, you would be capable of casting it. As such, I'd learned quite a few of these spells from Lorraine, and I was now a step ahead of Alize in that department. But I'd only known these spells for a short time, so I wasn't used to casting most of them and still had many unnecessary motions and delays in execution.

If I had to cast Linpio over and over again, though, fighting on my own was preferable, if only because it was easier on my reserves. While I was sure the amount of mana used would decrease should I become more used to the spell itself, it wasn't something I could master today or tomorrow.

"Don't you have any other means of attack, Edel?"

Unable to think of a solution, I decided to directly ask Edel for his opinion. While fighting by myself seemed the most optimal alternative, I realized it was also imperative for me to observe Edel's tactics on the field. The possibility of us coming up with some sort of combination attack was well worth considering. If anything, I should continue observing how Edel took on these weaker monsters, then consider what positions and attacks I could use should I enter the fray. I wanted some time to think. Edel, too, seemed to pause at my words, as if giving them some thought. Without warning, he jumped up, staring at the fallen goblin corpse...then fired something at it. Almost instantly, a huge gash made its way across the goblin's corpse.

"Magic...? Is this magic, Edel?"

I received a mental affirmation. To think Edel had mastered the use of offensive magic before his master... I couldn't help but feel some degree of annoyance.

Is some credit for your master too much to ask, I briefly thought. There were, however, some differences between magic used by monsters and the magic used by humans. Broadly speaking, they were both the same—phenomena materialized with willpower and mana. But humans built magic up as a sort of structure, understanding and building upon it, basically casting spells with the aid of incantations. In the case of a monster, mana was often instinctively turned into some sort of phenomenon directly. Most monsters were like this, although the intensity of said magic did vary. More humanoid monsters, such as goblins and vampires, were known to use something that more closely resembled the magic system of humans.

That said, most monsters were probably born with this instinctive knowledge of mana conversion. For example, the reason why a goblin was able to fight on equal footing with a grown man despite being half his size was due to the subconscious activation of a strengthening magic reinforcing its body. Similarly, there were tales of vampires being able to charm a weak-willed human just by looking into the human's eyes, convincing the human to serve them. This, too, was an application of magic—a charm spell cast with its eyes.

In other words, Edel may have picked up some of this mana-to-phenomenon ability somewhere along the line. While normal puchi suri were capable of nothing more than a sort of bodily reinforcement similar to that of goblins, elemental evolutions of mice were a little different. Take, for instance, a fire puchi suri, the fuu suri. It was capable of breathing small but functional fireballs from within its body, despite never having been taught how to use magic. Even so, these simple spells monsters were naturally capable of casting were by no means overwhelming in power. A vampire's Eyes of Charming, a fuu suri's tiny fireball, a dragon's breath attack… They were all the result of certain specialized organs in the eyes or throat of the creature. It was due to the presence of these organs that said attacks were effective or powerful. Even if you were to assume a monster knew all the appropriate structures and incantations for a spell, and hence became capable of casting magic, it would still be best served by bodily enhancement spells.

With Edel, the utilization of mana was of no import. Since he was a puchi suri with no specialized organs whatsoever, he shouldn't have been able to do what he had just done. If I had to guess, some physical changes had overcome Edel the moment I had evolved into a lesser vampire. Strictly speaking, he was probably no longer just a simple puchi suri. At least, that was my educated guess. As for where exactly this change had manifested itself in Edel's body… Well, a simple glance at him was enough for me to see it, really.

Edel looked very much like me.

Put plainly…he'd grown some sort of wing-like structure.

But of course, they weren't shooting out of his back. If anything, he'd grown some membranes on his underside, stretching from his underbelly to his hind legs. Much like a flying squirrel. I assumed he was capable of gliding should that membrane be pulled taut.

Curious, I asked for a demonstration, and, unlike me, Edel was able to fly relatively easily. The structure of his flight membranes were strange to say the least, but he was capable of not only gliding but also silently hovering in place. Compared to my hovering, violently darting, and torch-capable wings, Edel's were clearly a cut above when it came to flying.

I felt like I could ponder the issue for more than an hour. How could this be? That the familiar would have higher specifications than its master? Was this the intent of the gods? Or perhaps some underlying, unexplainable logic of the world?

I felt my faith dwindling.

Even so, I didn't feel that my divinity had diminished in any way. Then again, the spirits that conferred their blessings upon me probably didn't desire faith or worship in the first place. I could never really know, of course. It was impossible to seek confirmation, given all the time that had passed. However…I did have some thoughts as to why Edel was able to maneuver so freely through the air.

Mainly, there was a difference in weight between Edel and myself. With my permission, he could even draw from the very same reserves of mana, spirit, and divinity that I possessed. If anything, Edel, who was only a sixth of my weight, most likely found it much easier to float about comparatively. This was why he was able to zip around as he pleased without paying too much attention to energy expenditure. Plus, Edel was born a monster, so command over his powers most likely came naturally to him.

How enviable.

As I was currently limiting the amount of resources Edel could receive, his movements didn't include too many aerial acrobatics. Should I increase the amount by a small percentage, however, Edel was sure to begin soaring through the air. To think that he, who had no tutor or lessons of any kind, was slowly becoming stronger and stronger... If anything, his growth had already hugely exceeded mine!

How terrible...

But, if Edel were capable of it, I, too, would be able to do the same, albeit with some practice. I'd do well to make a mental note of that particular direction of self-improvement...

Amidst my contemplations, I realized I should have Edel show me the magic he'd just used. While I'd no longer have much work to do should Edel become any stronger than he already was, I couldn't deny that he was a valuable asset, and I couldn't complain about this recent turn of events. In any case, I had to understand his raw attack power, his mana usage, his range and spread, and if Edel was capable of using any other type of magic.

"I suppose we should search for a goblin or slime..." I suggested, with the intent of conducting our experiments on the unsuspecting monster. But Edel refused, instead mentally communicating to me that he wished to demonstrate his prowess on an orc.

Now, orcs weren't weak. And judging from Edel's movements as he fought goblins and slimes, I felt taking on an orc would be a little too much for him at this point.

"Would that be prudent, Edel? Orcs are nothing like goblins or slimes."

Edel responded simply, that should he ever be in danger, all I had to do was jump in and help him.

Honestly… Who is the master here, Mister Mouse, was what I thought…but I supposed such an experiment wasn't entirely unreasonable. Even if Edel had grown stronger and was now capable of using offensive magic, I was still unmistakably stronger in terms of fighting strength. I guess the fact that Edel still depended on me was something.

Exasperated, I no longer knew what I should be saying.

"…All right. We'll find us an orc, then," I said to Edel, who was currently mounted on my head, as I continued my descent to the next floor.

I could see the setting sun in the distance. It drowned the world in crimson. These sunset colors would inevitably give way to a world of darkness, but this was hardly a mysterious sight. If anything, it was quite a mundane one, repeated again and again on a daily basis…

At least, that's what anyone would have said…assuming they weren't deep inside a dungeon.

"Feels pretty strange, right…?"

And yet here we were, on the second floor of the New Moon Dungeon.

It was nowhere near evening yet; in fact, the sun was probably brightly shining high in the sky outside the dungeon's confines. It was plain to see that the passage of time within the New Moon, and perhaps dungeons in general, didn't align with that of the outside world. While I'd heard tales of it before, this was the first time I actually felt a dungeon's floor shift time zones, seeing as the previous floor felt perfectly in sync with the world outside.

If I had to guess, night fell upon this floor when the sun rose in the outside world, and vice versa. This was probably a normal occurrence in this particular dungeon, though. Walking to a floor that had yet to have daylight was one thing; walking to a new floor in pitch-black darkness was quite another. To most adventurers, this would be a most troubling thing, but there were many ways to go about the situation. For example, a particularly skilled mage could easily cast a spell that granted them night vision. However, most adventurers would simply give up then and there.

I supposed we were unlucky today; I had arranged to return at night, which would be when the sun rose on this floor. But on the other hand, I was lucky enough to be here at this point in time. It was now evening, and I still had ample light for vision and combat. Though, even if the sun should set, my eyes were of a special make. I found I could still see well enough at night; I could see much further than a regular human. If anything, the vision of an orc was closer to that of a human. As such, this situation was to my advantage since it was easier to fight an orc in the dark.

Now how would Edel fare? Since he was my familiar, his vision at night should be improved.

"Orc... orc... orc. Where would one be?" I hummed, as if singing some sort of strange incantation while I plodded along on the second floor of the New Moon.

Around me were forests and plains under a natural-looking sky. It looked so wide that it was impossible to tell where this sky ended. I'd heard adventurers could occasionally discover a place on the floor where the sky stopped, but also of instances where they could never seem to find it, no matter how hard they tried. All this was supposedly normal.

While orcs were quite different from your average human, normal orcs tended to roam in groups, or at least exhibited enough intelligence to flock in small numbers. As such, locating one orc would quickly lead to the rest. Conversely, if an adventurer were to be discovered by an orc, they would most likely have to contend with a few others at the same time. As such, adventurers usually progressed cautiously in these parts.

I, on the other hand, was currently seeking such a situation. Of course, if a stronger type of orc appeared in vast numbers, it could very well spell trouble, but this was merely the second floor. Such monsters had no reason to be appearing in these parts. But… it was still possible for a single, special monster of some sort to appear on the second floor. Should such a thing ever happen, all I had to do was run.

Perhaps it was due to everything going so well recently that I'd almost forgotten, but the reason I was how I was currently was all due to an unfortunate encounter with the pinnacle of all monsters: a legendary dragon. Such special monsters could very well exist, since I'd run into one before.

Again, I reminded myself to be careful. If I was ever forced into a situation where I had to draw my sword, I could calculate my chances of victory in that moment. If it was impossible for me to win, all I had to do was run, and that would be a victory in and of itself.

"Orc… orc… Hmm? Huh?"

I turned my head abruptly, suddenly assaulted by a strange feeling.

Something was…off.

What is it, exactly, I wondered, only to realize that my head felt unnaturally light.

Raising a hand up to my head, I finally realized what was missing. That which had been there before was no longer present…

Edel was gone.

Where's he gone off to…?

I sharpened my senses, conducting a search of the area. Due to the connection we shared, some degree of focus was all I needed to pinpoint his location. Upon doing so, I sensed a presence near the entrance of the forest. Exasperated, I approached the destination.

"Edel… I told you you shouldn't…"

I stopped short as I parted the undergrowth.

"…Braaaagh!!!"

"Gububu! Buruuuu!!!"

"Gigibu! Buuuruuuu!"

Nonsensical sounds greeted me. Surrounding Edel were three orcs, seemingly preoccupied with their conversation. Their weapons were drawn.

You're in quite the tough spot there, huh, Edel…?

Thinking so, I decided to act like any master would. I was about to intervene when I stopped dead in my tracks. My eyes hovered to the orcs' weapons and armor, which were made of a metallic material.

This was worse than I thought. These were no normal orcs…

They were orc soldiers.

Orc soldiers were a type of powerful orc, a step above the normal orcs commonly found in the dungeon. They were twice as big as normal orcs, and had equipment forged from metal. Those were their primary defining traits. There were also the orc kings and orc generals, monsters that were much stronger than the typical metal-armed orc soldier. However, those monsters hardly appeared on shallower floors and wielded visibly different weapons.

While the orcs surrounding Edel were armed with metallic weapons, their equipment was mostly made of bronze, or metals tainted with various impurities. In addition, their equipment didn't look particularly sophisticated. Compared to those creatures, an orc general could very possibly wield a mithril weapon—a truly fearsome thought.

An orc general also possessed a fair amount of skill on top of its unique weapon. Common wisdom on the matter stated that only a Platinum-class adventurer would be able to take it on. It was quite monstrous. To make matters worse, orcs of a higher caliber often dominated and ruled over those weaker than themselves. Depending on just how strong the orc in question was, one could expect the orcs under its command to be stronger and more numerous. In the case of an orc king, it could very well control every single orc in its territory, and I could hardly think of anything more fearsome than that.

Of course, even an orc soldier had some degree of commanding leadership; only a little, but some nonetheless. They, however, would only be able to lead normal orcs, and only one or a few of them at that.

Finally, their cries were capable of summoning more of their kind, the sound echoing far across the stratum. Taking too long to defeat them could be potentially fatal. If you were pursued by a large group of orcs, escape would be extremely difficult.

"...Edel!"

This was why I drew my sword, running toward the orc soldiers that surrounded Edel after a short series of thoughts. The message was simple: we had to defeat these enemies as quickly as we could. Edel agreed mentally, squeaking as he did so.

"Chu! Chu!"

With a series of squeaks, Edel started drawing upon my reserves of power, and I loosened my grip on just how much he could take. If I were too careless, Edel could very well absorb everything from me. While I'd thought to be a little more stingy over it, now wasn't the time for such concerns. Perhaps it was because they detected the change in our presence, but the orc soldiers no longer saw Edel as prey. They, too, readied themselves for combat, assuming battle stances.

But the orcs were far too slow. Already up close and personal with the monsters, I picked out the most arrogant orc soldier among them—the leader perhaps—and quickly thrust my blade at the nape of its neck. I'd thought it was a solid ambush, but even so, the orc soldier raised its sword and deflected my blow.

You're pretty good…

Ending it all with a single quick attack was too much to ask for. However, this was only the case if I was fighting alone.

While the orc soldier had turned toward me and deflected my strike mere moments ago, its expression was now one of marked confusion. But of course it would feel that way. It had been looking in my direction, but it was now looking straight up at the sky, as if it had been somehow launched through the air.

The reason for the orc soldier's sudden change in perspective was because Edel had slammed into one of its legs with his signature body slam, tripping the orc and causing it to fall backward. Although it had a giant body far greater than that of any man, it paid an equally heavy price for its metallic equipment. Its body, weighted down by these implements, toppled over almost hilariously upon losing its balance. Down it went, its head hitting the ground. The orc soldier, as if understanding that it was now at a disadvantage, attempted to get back up…but it was too late. My sword was once again at its neck, ready to strike.

37

Now prone and in a clumsy position, the orc soldier wasn't able to draw its own weapon in time. With a single, smooth motion, I beheaded the monster, cleanly separating its head from its body. With its head now gone, a fountain of blood dramatically spurted forth from its neck. I couldn't help thinking that it was such a waste. Quite the delicious meal, I would think, but the battlefield was hardly a place where one could idly sit and sip on a fresh fountain of blood.

All this transpired in but a few seconds. The two remaining orc soldiers, however, quickly understood what had happened and moved to attack us. Fortunately, the orc that Edel and I had just slain was most likely the leader of this motley crew, just as I'd predicted.

For a moment, it seemed like the orcs were wondering which one of us to take on, Edel or myself. Almost immediately, however, they split up, one coming after each of us.

Edel and I could not have asked for a better outcome. After all, I valued speed and technique more than strength, and Edel was of a smaller physique. The last thing we wanted to go against was an enemy with a numbers advantage. If only one orc came at each of us, fighting them would be very much doable. In fact, it was even possible for us to defeat them alone.

An orc soldier rushed at me with its sword raised, as if to strike. I made a quick step toward its center, landing a hit on its hand. It wore a metallic glove, and my blow failed to cut the orc's hand off outright. It did, however, succeed in disarming it, the impact causing the orc soldier to drop the sword it had been holding. Panicking, the orc soldier attempted to pick up its sword, but I had no intention of letting it do so. I struck out at the orc again with a quick thrust, not allowing it to retrieve its weapon. The orc soldier seemed to anticipate this, bending its body downward and almost ducking as it narrowly avoided my blade. It then proceeded to laugh and snort, as if to mock me. *Not the best course of action for this particular orc*, I thought.

As the orc soldier attempted to stand, I gave the sword it dropped a solid kick, sending it flying through the air. The sword, sailing in a straight line, embedded itself in the back of the other orc soldier who was currently locked in combat with Edel. Not a deep wound, of course, but even so…

"Bugii!"

Quite the cry of pain, I'd say—and yet another mental affirmation from Edel. "Doin' good," he said.

What are you now, mouse? My superior?

No matter. Though it was now completely disarmed, the orc soldier seemed intent on fighting to the death. It raised its fists and adopted a fighting stance. The monster was nothing more than a pig on two legs, yet it had the fighting spirit of a true warrior. It was something I could appreciate.

Even so…it was precisely because of this that I couldn't go easy on my opponent. Without any hesitation, I rushed the orc soldier, unleashing another thrust of my sword. The orc, now without any means of defense, attempted to block the blow with its gloves. It was a desperate attempt, but alas, the monster didn't have quite enough reach. With a sickening crack, my blade made contact with its head, fracturing the orc soldier's skull.

Some people would probably say the brain matter of an orc was delicious…but having to take that into consideration while fighting would be difficult. If I'd put more power into that blow, I could have finished it then and there, but the search I was on today was far from over. At the very least, I'd leave the head and brain of one orc intact… That would just have to do.

Regardless, monsters were tough creatures. The orc soldier was still moving, despite its now-fractured head and exposed brain.

Being partially lobotomized, it no longer had the mental capability to coordinate an attack. Instead, it was flailing around in place, its movements messy and careless.

I should finish it, I thought, raising my sword for one more strike.

As expected, beheading a monster was the quickest way of neutralizing it completely, so I did just so.

It was finally over.

This was still quite different from slaying a normal orc, but even I couldn't deny the growth I exhibited. To think a day would come where I'd be able to slay orc soldiers with ease... I'd have never believed it, even if I'd been told as such in life.

Suddenly...

Thud!

I turned in the direction of the loud sound. Edel had just finished his fight with the other orc a short distance away, the sound emitted being the finishing blow. As if heeding my previous wish, Edel had slain the orc not with a spinning body tackle, but with magic, cleanly severing its head from its throat. I stared as its head went rolling, coming to a stop as its large body collapsed onto the ground. The orc soldier was now very much dead.

A puchi suri slaying an orc soldier with its own power... No matter how I phrase it, no one will believe such a tale...

Such thoughts flickered across my mind as I stood, surveying the carnage before us.

And now it was time for dissection; the orc soldiers had to be adequately taken apart. Given that these orcs were a cut above their normal orc brethren, the taste of their flesh was almost guaranteed to be just as high quality.

You would usually only encounter orc soldiers at the tail end of the second floor or on the third floor of this dungeon. So why would three of these monsters appear here of all places, then…? All things considered, I supposed it wasn't an impossible occurrence. Perhaps they'd evolved much like I had, with time and experience. That was the logical assumption at least.

The same could be said for their equipment and weapons. Salvaged from fallen adventurers, perhaps. Orcs did have some degree of intelligence after all, so they'd be capable of that at the very least.

As I removed the metallic equipment from the orc carcasses, I quickly became aware of the numerous amounts of stitches on the bodies. In addition, some holes appeared to have been punched through parts of the carcasses. If the orcs hadn't evolved, then there was the possibility they could have traveled up from a deeper floor. But the likelihood of that was somewhat small. Dungeon monsters weren't known to stray from the floors they belonged to, let alone move freely to other floors.

The concept of what a floor was, however, was a mostly human definition. As such, the separation between one floor and another could sometimes be vague. You also had to take into account the actions of the monsters in question. Maybe it was out of territorial concerns or some other inexplicable reason, but most dungeon monsters were limited to a certain range of movement—what people define as "floors." There were no known cases of a monster wandering outside of this seemingly predetermined range. In fact, there were cases where the division between floors was visible to the naked eye. Monsters behaved as if they couldn't see such a division at all, and acted in a similar fashion.

Orc soldiers in the New Moon Dungeon, in turn, mainly lived on the fourth and fifth floors, and they weren't known to leave these areas. There were exceptions, of course, where in rare cases, a monster could move past this boundary or somehow cross between floors, eventually ending up on a floor markedly different than its normal habitat. The orcs that we'd just encountered may have very well done something similar. Though that was neither here nor there, really…

In some cases, a phenomenon known as a "flood" or "surging wave" could happen, causing monsters from within a dungeon to spill outside its confines. Unless something like that happened, however, monsters leaving their floors was highly abnormal. Sightings of monsters from lower floors like this were often thought of as premonitions, indicators of an upcoming flood or surge. I supposed there was some truth in that, so I made a mental note to inform the guild of what I'd seen upon my return. Not a compulsory thing to do, of course, but I should at least have a word with Sheila.

At the very least, this was by no means a dire situation. If a flood was indeed upon us, the signs would be much more visible. Floods were said to occur once every decade or two, and the last time one happened, even I was made to participate in the defense of Maalt. I didn't really know much else, given that I wasn't near the outskirts of any dungeons at the time.

However, from the rumors I'd heard, monsters from relatively deep floors were found roaming on the first floor. The actual flood happened about two days after that sighting. As such, even if what I'd just witnessed was a sign of a coming flood, it wouldn't happen for at least a week, if not a month. Time was a luxury we had. If such an event would come to pass once more, all I had to do was join in with the rest for the defense of Maalt, which should be sufficient in preventing the town from suffering huge losses. That was how Maalt survived all the past occurrences.

Either way, there was something else I should be doing now—namely, the gathering of materials.

Weapons and equipment for Alize...

I recalled Lorraine's list. The materials she'd asked for were magic crystals from monsters inhabiting the third floor or deeper, and wooden materials from a shrub ent. While there were many types of catalysts, the most famous among them was undoubtedly the wand. It was also faster to craft, which was more than enough for beginners at the art.

Eventually, Alize may need worn catalysts, such as a ring or a bracelet, but crafting such items would require a generous amount of coin. Due to the intricate nature of crafting worn catalysts, Lorraine settled for the wand, which was enough for our purposes now, or so I was told.

Although we'd taken Alize as our disciple, there was no guarantee she was going to become an adventurer. As such, it'd be best not to burden her with unnecessary debt. So long as I fetched some third-floor or deeper magic crystals and materials from a shrub ent, Alize might very well be able to craft the required catalysts herself.

The main consideration in this entire matter was if I could even take down a shrub ent... I'd never actually taken on that monster alone. I'd done the adequate reading at Lorraine's, in addition to having her answer any questions about the monster's capabilities, but it didn't take long for me to realize that it was by no means an easy opponent. While dealing with strong but simple monsters like orcs was somewhat straightforward, shrub ents were a wood elemental of sorts, so it wasn't easy coming up with a strategy to deal with them.

Though I was equipped with an undead body and physique and shouldn't suffer too many ill effects, I couldn't quite gauge the difficulty of the encounter until I actually fought it myself.

I continued pondering as my hands dissected carcass after carcass. Before I knew it, I was already done. The magic crystals had been harvested, and the neat cuts of orcish meat for self-consumption and sale were clearly marked, wrapped, and placed in my magic bag. If I overloaded my bag now, I'd have no space for the shrub ent materials later on, let alone other materials I might find on the way... So I finished gathering up the last of what materials I did need.

"We should get going, Edel," I said, setting out into the dungeon once more.

Next was the third floor. Remaining cautious as we continued on was the only thought in my mind as I walked forward.

"...Perhaps even more troublesome than the second floor's veil of night..." I said upon entering the third floor.

Stretching out before my eyes was what appeared to be an infinite ocean of trees. Looking up, we could tell there was a source of light from above. Small rays leaked through the greenery, but it was by no means bright. The path that Edel and I were advancing on had as much illumination as a small torch could provide. Not to mention our surroundings were pitch-black. The trees around us had grown so tall that they effectively blocking out most of the light from above. Even so, this was hardly a problem for us since we both had eyes better suited to seeing in the dark.

The problem was something else entirely. The branches of these huge trees grew and spread in all sorts of directions, obscuring our view. Regardless of whether we could see well at night, having an actual, material obstruction blocking our line of sight was something else altogether. While our eyes also had the ability to identify a living creature by its body temperature, that ability also seemed highly unsuited for this, so there simply didn't seem to be a use for it.

"Kii kii!!"

A voice rang out behind us. Reflexively, I drew my blade. Something descended to the forest floor right where we'd been standing moments ago.

It was...what appeared to be a monkey.

It was a slim monster, not particularly large, commonly known as the kesem kofu. Many lived on this particular floor. Their population was numerous, much like the slimes and goblins on the first floor.

But one couldn't really consider these monsters weak. This was the third floor, so monsters here were adequately cunning. You could no longer come out on top simply by rushing headfirst into an encounter, sword drawn.

"...Hunh!"

Upon drawing my sword and turning to face the kesem kofu before me, I felt a presence behind me, and I immediately lowered my head. A slight movement of air alerted me to the fact that something had just passed over my head. Turning around, I saw another one of the beasts hanging upside-down from a vine, claws at the ready. It had been attempting to swing at my head just moments before. Having failed once, the monster appeared to understand that a second attack would lose the element of surprise. The kesem kofu nimbly climbed up the vine it had descended upon and was soon lost in the canopy.

Focusing, I soon noticed the presence of many beings around us. It seemed like the kesem kofu didn't attack alone—that much we understood very clearly.

"Watch yourself, Edel," I said, only to receive a similar mental note from my familiar.

Considering that Edel was a mouse and probably didn't seem like anything other than a snack for the monkeys of this floor, I considered his answer sufficiently reassuring.

All things considered...there really were quite a lot of them. If there were just two, or perhaps three of them, we could have easily slain them without too much effort. From what I could sense however, there were at least 40 of the beasts currently surrounding our position. With the sheer amount of kesem kofu present, another attack was to be expected. This was compounded by how they jumped and swung from branch to branch. I found the situation quite difficult.

This was by no means the first time I'd fought in a forest. In the past, I'd set off on gathering trips to nearby forests, taking on goblins and slimes. Worst-case scenario, perhaps an orc would appear. But this? Monsters that moved freely through the branches, utilizing the terrain to launch surprise attacks? I had no experience dealing with such foes. I had done research prior to arriving at the third floor, gathering information on kesem kofu beforehand, but seeing the monster in person was another thing altogether. Nothing in the descriptive passages I read could compare to what I was currently seeing.

For starters…it was difficult to get a grasp of our surroundings. No matter how hard I looked, all I could see were shadows and branches. The monsters moved quickly, and I just as quickly lost sight of them.

Strictly speaking, the correct way to go about this was to infuse yourself with mana or spirit, then conduct a search of the surrounding area. However, I was still a beginner when it came to learning how to channel mana properly, and I didn't know many spirit techniques besides simple bodily enhancements. Something like sensing the surroundings or sharpening one's senses was currently not doable. I lacked the technique, and perhaps even the innate talent for such things. My divinity, too, didn't seem to do very much for me in this case. I supposed there was nothing more I could do, other than rely on instinct.

Dodging the attack of yet another kesem kofu by the breadth of a hair, I swung my sword, but I could hardly get any attacks in; their movements were simply too irregular. The way they descended from those vines was most irritating.

Should I just set this entire forest ablaze?

Hmm… Perhaps not. If I started a fire here, I would no doubt cremate myself in the process. I really didn't want to become a skeleton again…

Honestly, it seemed like the only way to handle this was to slice at the vines in question—reduce their length, so to speak. A grueling task, especially when I could be attacked from any angle at any moment…but I supposed there was no other way around it. At the very least, I wanted to disrupt their coordinated assaults, but that was probably a little too much for me at this point in time. Even if I did somehow climb up a tree, there was no way I could catch up with them.

I continued to worry about the issue, when suddenly…

"Chu!!!"

With a familiar squeak, Edel infused a pair of his limbs with mana before bolting up a nearby tree at an astounding speed, his claws digging into the bark. To think he was capable of something like that… I was genuinely surprised, if only because it was a feat I couldn't duplicate. Even if I were to try channeling mana into my feet, walking up a tree in that manner would be remarkably difficult. If I had to guess, Edel had probably strengthened his claws, giving him more friction to achieve such speeds. If I were to try anything similar, a slender tree would most likely snap after I had taken a few steps. Edel was able to do what he did because of his small size.

Unable to do much else, I continued dodging the attacks of the kesem kofu swarm on the ground, all the while slicing off what vines I could see in a most boring manner.

"…Kii!" "Ki kiii!!!"

With a few high-pitched wails from above, a kesem kofu fell, hitting the ground with a resounding thud. Numerous scratches had been carved into the monster, making it clear that this was Edel's doing.

However, those scratches were by no means fatal. Upon hitting the ground, the monster attempted to get up and scurry into the trees once more. I wasn't so kind as to let this opportunity slip. With a burst of speed, I closed the distance, bringing up my weapon for a two-handed swing.

I swung with such impunity because one could hardly harvest any useful materials from a kesem kofu. Its skin was thin, and its fur was hard and spiky; there was hardly a use for either material. They also tasted quite bad and couldn't really be eaten. The only thing that could be recovered from them were magic crystals.

The magic crystal of a kesem kofu was next to its heart. So long as I didn't direct any careless swings at that region, retrieving the crystal was relatively simple. A large wound in any other location hardly posed an issue.

I followed up on Edel's advance, finishing off the kesem kofu that continued to fall. Finally, he made his descent, landing in a small clearing where none of the beasts had fallen. He'd landed with an audible thump, but it appeared he was largely unhurt. He'd balled himself up, most likely using the considerable amount of fat on his body as a sort of cushion to absorb the impact.

In any case, I was glad that Edel was unhurt.

I did not, however, bear witness to anything that he'd done. I decided to ask him, only for him to inform me that he'd had quite the battle up in the branches. While I hadn't seen him in action, I could tell from the wounds left on the carcasses that Edel had put in a considerable amount of effort.

Since I'd largely been solo adventuring for most of my life, I wasn't used to this division of roles. I supposed Edel was quite useful, depending on the enemy's characteristics. Needless to say, it was impossible to know what waited for us ahead. I made a mental note to train myself for these situations in the future so that I could have a viable course of action should I be fighting on my own.

In any case, it was now time to move on to the dissection. As we were only harvesting magic crystals this time around, it didn't take long for me to finish my task. In the end, there were only about ten or so kesem kofu, and they ultimately didn't pose much of a threat.

Though, having kesem kofu ambush us time and time again would indeed prove tiresome. If anything, I should have Edel remain on alert and scan the surroundings, as we advanced on routes without the annoying monsters as much as possible.

I had to search for a shrub ent and harvest the materials required so Alize and I could each craft a wand of our own. As for the magic crystals… In the worst-case scenario, we could use some harvested from the kesem kofu.

Honestly speaking, though, I would have preferred a crystal of higher quality. Crystals harvested from kesem kofu were the least impressive on the third floor of the New Moon since they were small, somewhat translucent, and didn't have much power in them. If I were to gather crystals, something more respectable would be preferred.

Lorraine did mention, however, that it would be preferable to use a magic crystal that wasn't from a shrub ent for our wands. This made sense from an alchemical perspective, as the crystal was commonly mounted on the top of the wand. Having a crystal from another monster would serve to greatly amplify one's magical output. Should a crystal from the ent in question be used, the mana within the wand would simply gather at one spot and stagnate, making the catalyst difficult to use. A well-balanced wand required adjustment and calibration by its crafter. Alize and I would be taught these skills in the process of making them of course, but the difficult part was actually gathering the materials from different monsters. In some cases, a wand crafted from a single type of monster was more efficient, but the basics called for some variation here and there.

Even so…

It was easier said than done, especially considering that this was the third floor. All I had to do was do my best. *Just one more floor, Rentt…*

All that said and done…it really was difficult locating a shrub ent. They were formidable opponents, so it made sense that finding them in the first place would be equally difficult. Especially in a dense forest like this, of all places. Once they'd blended into their surroundings, it'd be all but impossible for an amateur to tell a shrub ent apart from a regular tree.

Shrub ents were the result of mana gathering and accumulating into a tree. In essence, they were monsters born from trees, so simply staring at them wouldn't do any good, seeing as they were basically the same thing. However, due to the nature of their creation and the mana accumulated in them, a seasoned mage would be able to tell one apart from a tree at a glance, but I wasn't capable of doing such a thing.

There were other ways, too. For instance, a magic item that resembled glasses and made mana slightly visible to the viewer. Said items were expensive though and would often only last for one use. To be precise, items like those were enchanted to only last for a day at most, and I had no intentions of paying for such a frivolous thing.

In the end, the search was proving difficult, and I found myself wishing that I'd bought such an item in the first place... A useless consideration at this point in time, no doubt.

This was why I turned to my final, most drastic solution. It left much to be desired in the safety department, but I had few choices left. My solution: I set about swinging my sword into everything, shrubs included. Now what would happen if one of my swings just so happened to hit a shrub ent? The outcome was quite predictable, really.

A shrub ent was originally a tree during some point in its life, but it was still turned into a monster. With the exception of a few notable examples, monsters were usually vicious and violent creatures. Should they be ambushed or struck by an object...

"...JYUUURRRRRRUUUVVVAAA!!!"

A rumbling sound, hardly one that a tree should be making, rang out from a relatively small, shrub-like plant that my sword struck. Under normal circumstances, branches and vines shouldn't be able to move, but they were now thrashing about, visibly alive. Soon enough, those very same vines swung at me like a whips, while the monster's branches extended and thrust out at me, as if they were wooden spears. It was evident to see that the tree in question was dead set on attacking me.

Originally, vines and trees didn't exactly get along. This seemed somewhat changed, however, probably a result of the tree becoming a monster. Both tree *and* vine were now taking aim at me, as if attempting to strangle and pierce me to death. I'd strongly prefer to not die by either of those methods...

A desire from the bottom of my heart, indeed. I continued chopping down the vines that struck out at me, all the while avoiding the sharp branches shooting in my direction with a few well-placed twists. Fortunately, what seemed to be the core part of the shrub ent appeared to be a thicker wooden trunk, so the monster couldn't move around freely.

The vines that I cut down slithered about like snakes before planting themselves into the ground, growing new roots where they could.

Why won't you die?

The vitality of these things is truly impressive, was what I thought to say, but an undead like myself really shouldn't be one to talk.

Would strangling and piercing me in multiple places even kill me? To kill a monster that had vampiric properties, its heart would have to be pierced by a weapon made of silver, or one coated with holy water—or so the folk stories said. In reality, lesser vampires were indeed dealt with in that specific way. If memory served, there were also a few cases of such measures successfully slaying middle vampires, too.

I'd heard no tales of vampires beyond that level being slain by such methods, however. In fact, I wasn't even sure if that was a possibility. I should just be more careful around silver and holy water.

Come to think of it, I was hardly affected by holy water before, so just silver then. But even then…I'd handled silver during some of Lorraine's experiments and didn't feel ill from doing so. I seemed to be very, very different from normal vampires, judging by all our differences. Did this mean I would die if strangled or pierced, then? I had absolutely no idea…

Disregarding my rambling thoughts on my own physique, I felt a bit relieved. I'd sliced off some of the monster's vines and branches, giving me some breathing room. The roots sprouting from the fallen vines seemed to grow at a slow pace, but their growth was still clearly visible. At the very least, they were growing much faster than a normal plant would. Would they grow into new shrub ents if I left them alone…?

More important was the monster before me. As its appearance suggested, a shrub ent was a tree that had become a monster— a moving monster tree, so to speak. A most vicious, hateful face had surfaced upon a particularly thick trunk, marking the core of the monster, perhaps. It was most disgusting and hardly a pleasant thing to look at. Vines were wrapped along its branches and trunk, and its eyes and mouth were illuminated by a dim light that flickered as it moved. It was a mystery as to when these appeared, whether it was when it was still a tree, or after it had become a shrub ent.

According to the tomes I'd read, some specimens of this monster type came with vines, and some others didn't. If I had to guess, this tree had probably been entwined with vines long before it evolved into a monster. The shrub ent before me, which was still thrashing around and attempting to impale me with sharp wooden branches, did have a bit of a white tone to its wood, so it had probably been a birch tree at first.

Regardless, I didn't have very much knowledge when it came to forestry and trees, so I had no way of ascertaining the suitability of this particular wood in wand-making. According to Lorraine's answers on the matter, any wood from a shrub ent would cause the output potential of a wand to increase. That much was visibly evident in how the monster was able to use its own body as weapons, branches, vines, and all.

I'd swung my sword with quite some force, but the tree didn't snap or break in half. I could infuse my weapon with mana or spirit to cut it down, but the same could be said for most wood materials. In other words, there was little need for me to worry about the wood's suitability or strength.

As for how much wood I actually needed... Considering we were making short wands, I couldn't see us using more than forty centimeters of raw material. I really didn't need any more than that. But with this being the case, I had a good mind to secure several specimens for this purpose since I couldn't spend too much time on a single monster.

From my repeated clashes with the shrub ent, one thing was clear: it didn't have any special means of attack. The most it did was flail its vines or attempt to pierce me with its branches, and maybe a body slam too, if it got close. That was all there was to it. So if it stuck to this routine, an all-out offensive seemed fit for my purposes.

Believing my assumptions to be true, I waited for the shrub ent's next attack. I neatly dodged the monster's flurry of branches as they flew toward me, slicing some of them off along the way. Closing the distance, I stabbed my sword deep into the monster's eye socket, an easy opening on its grotesque trunk-face.

The space behind the monster's face seemed hollow and empty, but there was more to it than that. To be precise, this empty hollow was the so-called main body of the shrub ent itself. The monster wasn't just a tree or some wooden bits; the true form of a shrub ent was that of an amorphous spirit housed within the hollow. That meant this particular monster had a glaring weakness. Under normal circumstances, you would strike at that particular part of the ent, but few individuals did so.

It was probably to be expected, though. After all, the so-called core of this monster was an immaterial spirit. A normal, physical attack wouldn't be capable of dealing much damage to it at all. But there was a purely physical way of taking down a shrub ent, by destroying its trunk outright.

The rationale for such attacks was that the spirit within a shrub ent was highly unstable and didn't have much of a grip on the material plane. Should the trunk that it possessed be destroyed, it would lose a medium to bind itself to, and in the process basically stop existing. Not exactly the best way to go about harvesting wood from an ent. Even if I didn't really need that much wood from the monster, I wanted to gather as many materials as possible. If we had any wood left over, it would sell for several times the price of normal lumber. Now, I always had "saving coin and making gold" on my mind, so I had no intention of destroying it physically. What, then, would you deploy against an immaterial opponent, impervious to physical attacks?

Mana and spirit were options. Unless an adventurer was armed with one of the two, fighting an immaterial foe was impossible. Usually, the most effective means of combating spirits was divinity. However, individuals who wielded divinity were rare, and there were no commonly known methods for slaying monsters with it.

Nonetheless, I already had a plan in mind. Burying my sword deep into its eye socket, I channeled and coated my weapon with mana. Almost immediately—

"GIGGGIIIAAAYAAA!!!"

A high-pitched wail blasted out from the shrub ent's somewhat disturbing mouth opening. As the wail subsided, a wispy, black substance wafted out from the ent's body, almost like a trail of smoke, before dissolving into the air and disappearing completely. With that, the light in the ent's eyes and mouth slowly faded. As the tension faded from its branches and vines, the monster collapsed, its body falling to the ground with a thud.

I supposed it was now slain.

The vines on the ground, too, stopped growing their roots as rapidly as before, returning to a more normal rate of growth. At the very least, I couldn't visually discern them growing from where I stood.

The shrub ent's main body, now on its side, was mostly unscathed. I could confidently say there were more than enough materials to be had off its lifeless shell. After conducting a quick scan of my surroundings and confirming there were no monsters in my immediate vicinity, I moved to collect the materials I'd come for.

Intermission: Rina Rupaage, Adventurer

Quite some time had passed since that most peculiar encounter. An encounter with a ghoul, a gentle one at that, with a series of complicated blue tattoos on its face. Rina's life should have ended then and there had it not been for the intervention of this most curious undead.

Thinking back on it, it was a most bizarre experience. In hindsight, it might have been nothing more than a dream. Rina had prepared clothing and a mask for the ghoul and was even complicit in tricking the guard at one of Maalt's gates to allow him passage. It was the first real adventure of her life. A most mysterious adventure at that—if anything, it almost seemed like a tall tale.

Even so…the more she thought about it… No. No matter how much she thought, Rina understood that letting an undead into the city was an unforgivable act. Rina did have common sense. However, she'd gone and done it, even with the understanding that it was a forbidden thing to do.

Her reasoning was that Rentt was supposedly not a bad person. Of course, had Rentt just been a normal undead of sorts, Rina would have never done what she did. In other words, she had developed a deep sense of trust for Rentt in the short time that they'd spent together. She'd never really experienced that before—trusting someone so deeply, that is.

Rina's father was strict. He went so far as to plan out her life for her, what she should and would do. Her mother wasn't any better, often criticizing her for a perceived lack of elegance the moment she opened her mouth. After that topic had been exhausted, her mother moved on to a seemingly endless tirade on potential suitors. One couldn't exactly say that Rina's parents loved her. They simply wouldn't listen, even if she insisted that she had things she wished to accomplish, things she wanted to do. The only one who would listen to everything she had to say was her brother, who was quite a few years her senior.

Rina wondered what her brother was doing…

Her brother, Idoles Rogue, was the eldest son of the Rogue family—Rina's rightful family, of course. He belonged to the elite First Brigade of the Kingdom of Yaaran. Having been born into a family of knights, Rina looked up to him and dreamed of becoming a knight, just like Idoles. That was how she wanted to live her life.

However, reality was…different. Female knights did exist in the Kingdom of Yaaran, but only to a certain extent. Her brother had even spoken of two female knights in the First Brigade who were both dispatched on the same assignments as their male peers.

But Rina's parents couldn't accept the fact that she looked up to her brother and aspired to become a knight herself. That was where the problems began.

Rina's father was rigid in his views. He didn't think women should aspire to be knights. Rina's mother similarly opined that women should be happy to be protected by a nice gentleman, and thought of that as a woman's ultimate form of happiness. As such, she refused to budge on the matter of arranging a marriage for Rina.

Despite this, Rina didn't completely think her parents were in the wrong. As nobles, her parent's views were more socially acceptable, if not seemingly correct. But then, why did her parents have to be this rigid? Was it not all right to let up just a little bit?

She wanted her parents to listen to her thoughts, and perhaps think about her future together. Just one conversation, if anything.

Rina's parents weren't of the same opinion. The only one who acted differently...was her brother. He listened to her thoughts intently. He thought of ways to deal with the situation and set about negotiating the affair with their parents. The outcome remained unchanged, however, as her parents refused to budge. Even so, Idoles did everything he could possibly do for her.

Now that matters had come to a head, Rina's brother laid her possible choices on the table. Plainly speaking, if she were to stay at home, she'd eventually, but surely, be married off to some unknown noble. That wasn't necessarily a bad thing, but Rina wouldn't have any of it, so her brother gave her one more suggestion: running away from home. But she would find it most difficult to become a knight under such circumstances, since she'd have to stand on her own two feet, all ties with her family severed. Having been born into such a family, Rina was raised in comfort, not knowing poverty or want. Could she stand on her own, and did she have the resolve for it? Her brother inquired as such.

Now, Rina wasn't completely ignorant of reality. She knew it would be a difficult choice to make. She also knew just how hard it was for a young girl to make a living on her own in a world such as this. While her parents wanted to protect her and prevent her from ever seeing the darker side of the world, Idoles was different. In fact, he often brought her to such depraved and terrible places. Whenever her parents left for some party or another, she and her brother would sneak out on such excursions, to suspicious backstreets and alleys full of lurking dangers. Rina would wear tattered clothes commonly worn by commoner girls, and he would dress up as a street punk of sorts. Together, they'd walk the streets and alleys.

Those days were an adventure in their own right. Rina remembered them with nostalgia.

Perhaps it was strange that her brother, raised in a noble family, would know those mean streets so well, even how to blend in. Finding it somewhat mysterious, Rina questioned him on the purpose of these excursions, and he explained they were to change her perspective, or at least to provide her with a new one. For her to see just how different the lives of commoners and nobles were, how difficult it could be. How the common folk had the courage and grit to live another day, all the while being uncertain whether they'd live to see tomorrow. Or even the means a woman would resort to if she had to live on no matter the cost; the means and methods that those cornered by desperation had turned to.

Of those who'd lost everything, and what eventually became of them…

Under normal circumstances, the daughter of a noble family would never bear witness to such scenes. If anything, it was normal for them to be locked away in their grand mansions, as if living a sweet, peaceful dream. In that regard, Rina's brother was different indeed.

He'd probably already seen that this would happen from the very start, that Rina would eventually step off the path planned for her… Or maybe that she'd eventually run away from home. Maybe it was because of this that he thought to educate her on the harshness of the world, the painful realities of it. Maybe then, she would give up…and if she didn't, then these experiences would prove to be important lessons.

In reality, those experiences were exactly what she'd needed in her life. Rina became an adventurer because she'd understood something: she had reserves of mana and spirit within her.

With some honing, she could very well make a living as an adventurer, which she'd found out upon joining her brother during those excursions. Most nobles were known to have notable reserves of spirit or mana in them, but Rina was a little special in that regard. Her reserves were much more significant. At the very least, she had enough mana in her to put her on equal footing with a fair amount of monsters, though she did need some study and practice. Spirit was something that was constantly honed by its user, as one usually increased their spirit reserves with significant amounts of training and effort. While it was difficult for her to capitalize on that from the get-go, she had more than enough mana within her for combative purposes.

In addition, Rina also learned basic swordplay and combat techniques from her brother, all in the hopes of becoming a knight. With some mana and combat techniques, one would be able to function as an adventurer, albeit at the bare minimum. Such was her understanding of the matter. This was why she'd made her choice.

After pondering the matter and discussing it with Idoles numerous times, Rina decided to run away from home.

A vague, ambivalent expression floated across her brother's face as she made her choice known. Even so, he didn't disapprove, instead offering his support, respecting that she'd made her own choice. Though he did remind her to contact him from time to time since her family wouldn't simply cease existing, no matter how far away she went.

Several days after the decision was made, Rina changed into some commoner clothing that Idoles had prepared for her, equipped some cheap weapons and armor, and with a few weeks' worth of traveling money, finally left her home. Rina would then, with her own two feet, make the journey to the adventurer's guild and register as an adventurer.

She'd taken this far too lightly. Rina was made aware of this unexpectedly early on in her career.

She'd learned combat techniques from her brother, an actual knight belonging to an elite order. She had some capabilities of her own as well, and she assumed that making a living at the guild would be easy. But her hopes were soon dashed.

For a few days, Rina accepted some simple, middling requests, saving what money she could as she scraped by. When that, too, became unsustainable…Rina heard of a certain town by the name of Maalt. With the risk of running into her parents quite high should she stay in the capital, Rina decided to head to Maalt. But she didn't have much of a pleasant experience upon her arrival there. Her beginnings there were equally difficult since Maalt was a rural border town. Staying alive was a fight in and of itself—that fact hadn't changed.

Her meeting with that particular undead was what finally put an end to those days.

The time Rina spent with Rentt was short, but interesting. To her, Rentt was a swordsman of considerable skill. She assumed his current appearance was due to some sort of special, unfortunate circumstance. Originally, he'd been an adventurer by the name of Rentt Faina. However, certain events happened, and he was like that when he awoke. Even Rina didn't believe his tale in the beginning, yet she somehow knew this strange undead wasn't lying. And so it came to be that she spoke to, cooperated with, and slowly began solving the problems that plagued him. She felt a sense of achievement, of accomplishment, as their plan for him to enter Maalt had succeeded.

However, Rentt immediately suggested they should part ways. It was quite a shock to her. But thinking back on it, she realized Rentt was simply looking out for her in his own way. After all, the punishment for conspiring with an undead, and eventually letting it into the city, was undoubtedly severe. She could be persecuted, hunted—or perhaps something worse.

It was only now that Rina understood why Rentt had distanced himself from her. He probably felt like he had no other choice. No— she knew even then, deep in her heart, why he parted ways. She just hated saying goodbye and refused to acknowledge this fact.

But with some time between now and then, and Rentt's teachings in her mind... Rina turned toward the future. He had listened to what she had to say on their journey and had given her many pieces of advice. Perhaps that, too, was the undead's way of looking out for her.

For instance, he informed her about what she could do to get herself out of her current, perilous situation as an adventurer. He gave her general directions, tips on useful hunting grounds, reputable merchants to trade with, methods of negotiation and haggling... Rentt taught her many things. If she put his advice to good use, she was sure she could continue making a living as an adventurer. She very much believed so.

Rina was now heading to the guild, adopting a completely different set of behaviors and motives. She would carefully analyze any given request and only take on those suitable to her skill level. She no longer viewed solo adventuring negatively, but instead she'd do what she could. Rina now understood that it was imperative to prove her own mettle, to demonstrate her own strength, before thinking of grouping up with others in a party. She also sought information on other parties from the receptionist, as well as knowledge on what other parties were looking for when it came to recruiting new members. Rina had been working without this knowledge this entire time. Though he had done his best to prepare her, her brother was a knight, so of course he didn't know much about the adventurer's guild, or the general situation and challenges adventurers would face.

This all changed upon her chance meeting with Rentt. Slowly but surely, Rina took on a variety of requests, gradually honing her combative capabilities. She also attended workshops held by the guild, to learn as much as she could and commit to memory what she absolutely needed to know. As a result, she continued taking on request after request, and her success rate slowly increased with time. Eventually, a missive came for her, asking if she belonged to any particular party.

A small party had inquired, made up of a boy and a girl, both around her age. But they'd already been promoted to Bronze-class and were supposedly skilled enough in what they did. One of them was a swordsman, and the other was a mage and healer. It was a well-balanced party.

After some discussion of the usual terms and conditions, Rina decided to become their third member.

Chapter 2: Materials for My Disciple's Weapon

After striking down the first shrub ent, I continued hunting others for a while. The previous one had mutated from a birch tree, and I assumed the wood I'd collected was of good quality. Even so, I wanted to gather several other types of lumber.

Although shrub ents were a type of tree-monster in general, they could mutate and materialize from a variety of trees. According to Lorraine, different types of lumber displayed different characteristics. Though she said she didn't have a specific type of wood in mind for this particular request, I decided to gather a few others either way, just to be sure. In the end, I'd collected lumber from ebony- and fir-based ents, which should be sufficient for my needs.

I also ran into a shrub ent that had previously been a grapevine of some sort. It broke apart when struck, showering me with a highly corrosive acid. It also threw acidic spheres, making it a very troublesome foe. I was, of course, immune to poisons of all types, but even I understood I could be burnt by acidic substances. Fortunately, the robes I was wearing appeared to be somewhat acid-proof, and I managed to shrug off the attack. But even then, I really didn't want to run into something like that again.

In fact, after that encounter, I decided to stop hunting ents altogether. If I were able to utilize magic, I'd simply fire a spell from afar, and in doing so safely discern between an ent and a regular tree. That, however, was impossible for me at this point. I also thought of asking Edel, eventually doing so, but it was futile in the end.

I was here for materials, and Edel only knew two spells: a blade of wind and a fireball. One would scar the lumber badly, and the other would burn the whole place down. Maybe it was still too difficult for Edel to control the output of these recently acquired spells? Either way, this could only be solved by working hard and learning proper magic in the near future.

While it was Edel who had first mastered how to channel and shape this power, this was probably due to his desire to assist me. There were many monsters that could blend into their surroundings, the shrub ent being just one of them, and it'd be most troublesome if I had no way of telling them apart should the need arise—other than clubbing them with some sort of object, that is. I may be many things, but I am not a caveman by any measure.

If you were in a place like the Water Moon Dungeon, such worries would be uncalled for. But the same couldn't be said for the areas beyond this floor. Progress was a good thing, yes, but monsters like that were worrisome. I supposed I just had to put my back into it.

I continued walking, and soon the forest opened up into a wide clearing. In the middle of it was something that shouldn't exist in a natural, real forest: a stairway leading down. Where exactly it led to was none other than the next level of this dungeon, the fourth floor.

That much was known to me instinctively. Thinking about it calmly, however, I realized I still didn't understand the reason as to why these dungeons were built. Who would have made such a place, and for what reason? Was it the work of the gods? Or perhaps the faeries? While there were many theories, the dungeons' existences remained one of the greatest mysteries of the world.

Now, I had no hopes of solving said mystery. That would be something left to someone like...Lorraine, perhaps.

My job was much simpler. All I had to do was defeat monsters, monsters much like the ones currently wandering around the stairwell.

While I'd been looking forward to exploring the fourth floor, it seemed the dungeon disagreed with my enthusiasm. Gathered and loitering around the stairwell were quite a few forest wolves.

Forest wolves, as their name might suggest, were wolf-type monsters that mainly lived in forests. They also inhabited the third floor. They were weak individually, since they were nothing more than slightly hairier wolves. But they were a danger when attacking in packs. The monsters themselves usually hunted as such; it was their nature. When quite a few of them were gathered, much like now, some of the wolves would howl, magically strengthening other monsters in the vicinity. They were every bit as worrisome as I'd mentioned.

To make things worse, there were five wolves before me. *What a hassle...*

But they had to be defeated if I were to proceed. They were blocking my path to the stairwell, after all, and running past them would be quite a challenge.

I did have a choice, however. I could simply return home for today and not proceed any further. Honestly speaking, I already had more than enough materials to create some wands: the shrub ent's lumber for the handle of the wand, and magic crystals from the fallen orc soldiers mounted on the top as catalyst mediums.

Due to the fact that orc soldiers were monsters commonly found on the fourth and fifth floors, materials harvested from them were adequate for the creation of a wand. But those orc soldiers had strayed far from their original floors, which caused the quality of their crystals to decrease...which fueled my desire to collect better magic crystals. We were making beginner wands, so materials of a slightly lower quality would suffice, but catalysts had a tendency to explode if they were synthesized from sub-par materials. I didn't want Alize to be using anything so dangerous. As such, I wanted to gather other types of magic crystals if possible… which landed me here.

Thinking about it more, I realized I could even use the magic crystal of a forest wolf. But I still couldn't return home; I'd yet to gather the materials for Alize's weapon. And since I'd already come all this way, I might as well return with some spoils from the fourth floor. Surely I'd be able to gather quite a few different materials there.

Taking all that into consideration, I had little choice but to defeat the forest wolves before me.

I placed a hand at my waist, drawing my blade. I channeled mana into my sword and body, strengthening them both. Forest wolves were monsters that relied on their speed. A solid first strike would surely influence the flow of battle afterward.

The first strike had to draw blood.

I slammed a foot onto the ground and raised my sword for a preemptive attack.

…Gyawaaan!!!

Slashed by my blade, the monster leapt away with a piercing cry. My target was none other than the largest forest wolf in the group. If I had to guess, this wolf was the alpha. I couldn't be sure though, so I decided to strike first. It appeared I was right on the mark.

The other forest wolves in the surrounding area heard the howl and entered a state of alert, glaring at me from where they stood. Then, they struck.

Though it wasn't a fatal wound, the monsters were annoyed that I'd gotten a hit in on their leader. Loyal, yes, but all too predictable. Their movements were easy to read, so I'd say this was a successful first strike.

I turned to the first incoming wolf and sliced into it, flinging it away with the weight of my blade. I did the same to the next. No matter how quick they were, I simply deflected their straight, head-on attack with a well-placed blow. There was no easier hunting than this—until the leader of the monsters soon noticed what I was doing.

With yet another loud howl, it alerted the other forest wolves.

I began to notice forest wolves had quite the thick hide. A single attack didn't really hinder them much. As expected of the New Moon Dungeon... The monsters here had a higher level of endurance, most likely because I was near the entrance to the fourth floor.

I'd slain the shrub ents somewhat easily because I just so happened to be able to pinpoint their weakness. You could say I had quite an advantage over them. In the case of these forest wolves, however... This was quite the difficult encounter.

After an assertive howl from their leader, they regained their calm. Their movements were visibly those of skilled hunters. They no longer gave me many openings to work with, so the situation was now that of a stalemate. If the battle were to stretch on like this, my stamina would surely wear out. For a moment, I thought of tossing Edel, who was currently perched on my shoulder and not fighting at all, toward the wolves as food. Edel's response was swift. "Don't even think of it" was the gist of his response. *I suppose I'll honor your request, mouse...*

In that case, I had no choice.

The solution was pork.

I reached into my magic bag and pulled out a slab of pork wrapped in a Maaltan Magnolia leaf—wrapped orc meat, in other words—and tossed it at the monsters. Since I couldn't use the mouse as bait, I'd use orc meat. Not a very imaginative plan, but orc meat was considered a delicacy to both humans and monsters.

As the meat's fragrance wafted past the forest wolves' noses, they let their guard down for just a moment. It was just what I'd been looking for.

I propelled myself forward in a familiar motion. Raising my sword, I channeled mana into the blade, aiming to land a decisive blow.

If I wanted to sever something, mana was the best candidate. I wanted to conserve my energy, so I limited the amount of mana I channeled into my blade. However, using mana to slice a hard object meant quite a bit of it would be used. Though, if my reserves of mana were emptied out in the worst-case scenario, I could just return home at that point.

The leader of the forest wolves, as if noticing I'd been waiting for this moment, quickly gave three short barks. Probably something to the effect of, "Don't be distracted by the meat!" A terrible thing to say, given that the leader itself was drooling at the scent of it.

Is orc meat really that delicious? Well, I guess it would be…

The wolves noticed a little too late, however. By the time their attention had returned to me, I'd already buried the blade of my sword into one of the monster's necks.

So far so good, but as expected…this flesh was hard. The endurance of these monsters was markedly different from those of the previous floors. If it were a goblin or a normal orc, this amount of mana would have been more than enough to cleanly remove either of their heads.

Perhaps it was a sign from the dungeon that the early floors with easily slain monsters ended here. But these monsters could be sliced up, so it wasn't impossible.

I tensed the muscles in my arm while increasing the amount of mana I channeled into my sword. With that, the impaled wolf froze. With a heavy sensation, the blade sank deeper into the forest wolf's flesh. I pulled the blade through with a swift motion, cleanly slicing through the monster's flesh. A dull thud—and the forest wolf's head was on the ground.

Monsters were much more resilient than they looked.

The wolf's head, now on the ground, spun violently this way and that, still staring in my direction as it met its end. Its body, too, remained standing for a short while, shivering as it did so. I suppose it couldn't live for much longer after being separated from its head, however, because it fell to the ground in a few seconds. The body was still, the head's eyes now closed.

…One down. Four more to go.

The battle was far from over, but it'd be much easier from here on out. After all, these particular forest wolves were used to hunting in packs of exactly five.

Why did I know this? Because there were now gaps in their patterns of attack. The timing of their approaches was visibly off. Their combination attacks had been relatively flawless before, so this new development made them significantly easier to deal with.

The forest wolves, surprised by how I'd aimed for the lapses between their attacks, didn't know how to react. In response, the leader, now visibly agitated, ground its fangs together before dashing straight at me.

We can end this right now.

I raised my sword once more, channeling mana into its blade as I aimed for the wolf's neck. If I let them reorganize themselves and regroup, the gap in their attacks would effectively disappear. Their pack of five was now a group of four. Now was the opportune time to strike.

To the wolf, however, me dashing in to take advantage of this chance may have been the opportunity they sought as well. If I let up on the attack now, I'd have to start fighting defensively, in which case, the battle was sure to drag on.

Forest wolves were known for their explosive potential, using quick, powerful strikes as their weapons. But they didn't have much in the way of stamina. They were stronger than a normal wolf, but they didn't have the capability to fight for more than tens of minutes, and definitely not hours with an adventurer armed with mana techniques. If I didn't finish this here and now, victory would depend entirely on when the wolves would tire out.

Well, then. Let's go.

Raising the sword above my head, I turned to the leader and unleashed a vicious downward swing. It, too, had a trick up its sleeve, because its fur began glowing a dim green. Was it channeling mana into its body? While I didn't know what it was about to do, I understood that the wolf was now fighting seriously. No... The fact that the monster was using this ability now—it could very well be its trump card.

I could feel a certain pressure emanating from the monster. This forest wolf was somewhat larger than the rest, possibly because it was the leader of these monsters.

But I couldn't lose here. I was still Bronze-class. I still had a long way to go to become strong enough to defeat an enemy like this almost effortlessly...

I focused intensely on that thought and brought the blade down on the forest wolf's neck. The blade dug deep, slicing straight through. I'd increased the amount of mana by almost 50 percent, hence the lack of resistance. It being the leader, I hardly expected to be able to defeat it with the same amount of strength.

The attack was successful, and I pulled my sword through what remained of its flesh. Its head was now falling toward the ground. I'd won, but—

It opened its mouth. With a resounding "woosh!" what appeared to be a green, shining blade flew out from the monster's gaping maw, flying straight at me.

Damn!

I panicked as I bent forward, attempting to dodge the attack. The green blade of wind narrowly missed me, almost grazing my cheek as it did so. Immediately after, a thunderous sound rang out from behind me—the sound of something splintering and breaking. Turning around, I witnessed a large tree fall on its side, sliced clean through by the spell.

Is it still alive...?

I should have noticed this upon slaying the very first forest wolf... But to think it could cast a spell in such a state. An unexpected development...

The leader's head was now silent, so I guessed that was its final attack. Even so, I had no intention of letting my guard down. I vowed to be cautious with the remaining three monsters. I had to be careful even after they were slain.

That said, the remaining wolves were now without a leader, and their movements were exceedingly easy to predict. They could no longer launch any combination attacks. All they did was rush at me in straight lines, hoping to get a good bite in.

I, in turn, simply cut them down one by one—it felt almost too simple. The difficulty of the encounter I'd complained about mere moments ago was nowhere to be seen.

In the end, I spent only a few more minutes defeating the remaining wolves. But I was now armed with firsthand knowledge of just how terrifying forest wolves that banded together in packs could be. With a few decisive swings, the battle met its end.

The carcass of a forest wolf provided an adventurer with quite a few usable materials. There was its magic crystal of course, but also the wolf's hide. In life, the wolves strengthened their skin and fur as much as they could, so much so that even the sharpest sword couldn't easily harm them. At a glance, the hide of a forest wolf was impossibly hard, but that very same hide was now surprisingly soft to the touch, having lost all its previous tension in death. The hide was smooth, its fur warm. One could fall asleep stroking it.

The pelts of forest wolves were in high demand, used in the manufacture of coats, rugs, carpets, and the like. They had to be carefully dissected and preserved since the pelts were worth a good sum of coin. While it couldn't be made into weapons or armor, it was still an important source of income.

Its fangs and teeth, however, could be processed into tools, so I'd be harvesting those, too. Its pelt was one thing, but the carcass of a forest wolf provided quite a few other useful materials too. It was most gratifying.

After I was done harvesting the appropriate materials, I dug a hole in the ground and buried what remained of the monsters. I could have left the carcasses there, yes, but I'd fought these wolves right at the entrance of a downward-leading stairwell. Doing so would inconvenience adventurers ascending from lower floors, and even adventurers currently in this area. I could hardly think of any adventurer who'd find a gathering of monsters at the top of a dungeon stairwell amusing.

Edel also helped with the process, scattering the lingering smell of fresh blood with his wind magic.

All that was left now were sprays of blood and scraps of meat on the ground, but there was little I could do about that. At the very least, such a small amount of blood and scattered scraps shouldn't attract a huge horde of monsters… Maybe ten or so at most. Adventurers heading up from deeper floors were usually extremely careful during their ascent. If the debris here really did attract a fair amount of monsters, said monsters would be visible from afar. Adventurers who couldn't defeat a large group would most likely give up and return home.

Basically, there were no longer any outstanding issues here.

Though I did need to remember what had happened here even as I descended to the fourth floor… It'd be all too foolish if I somehow walked into a monster horde of my own making, not knowing they were there, and perished in the process.

A potential horde of monsters on the third-floor stairwell… A potential horde of monsters on the third-floor stairwell… A potential horde of monsters on the third-floor stairwell…

Good. I've said it three times now.

Still muttering the reminder, I made my way down to the fourth floor, taking care to tread slowly and carefully.

Stepping out from the stairwell, I was greeted by what appeared to be a huge mountain made out of strong, weathered rock. We were now on the fourth floor. The mountain was floating, a gigantic piece of rock casually suspended in the air. Surrounding the surreal sight was nothing but empty, bottomless space.

The place I stood was linked to the giant floating mountain by a single path. More precisely, the end of the descending stairwell was supported by a small floating rock…small compared to the mountain, anyway. The rock was approximately the size of a three-story house.

Both were very rocky floating objects indeed, and no other path could be discerned from my position.

What would happen if you fell into that seemingly bottomless space...? Those who knew had never returned, or at least it seemed that way. Of course, you could probably fall into the bottomless darkness and see what laid within with your own eyes.

Jokes aside, there were indeed a few fools who floated a robe or something similar down into the empty space. But ultimately, they couldn't tell just how far down the space went. It appeared even floating spells and magic items were disabled, which made it impossible for you to investigate the apparently bottomless point.

Now, I myself had wings, yes, but there was a high chance I could fall either way... I didn't have the guts to try it out. I did, however, know that the fourth floor's main segment was that very same mountain I was currently looking at, suspended in mid-air.

The mountain was like a floating island of sorts. I found it most mysterious that something like this could exist in the dungeon, but I supposed it was too late to be saying such things.

To begin with, the mountain was at a much higher plane of elevation than the stairwell I'd just exited from... You could almost say that the platform the stairwell was on was floating in the opposite direction. Besides the stairwell that extended straight into the floating rock, there was nothing else around the platform. It was a mystery how such a stairwell could even lead an adventurer back to the third floor.

As I stood absentmindedly admiring the strange scenery of the fourth floor, I noticed something in the distance faintly moving along the path leading up to the floating mountain.

Those were, of course, monsters.

I'd heard rumors of this, about how they'd rush up to any adventurer entering the fourth floor, as if to welcome them.

What an unnecessary welcome.

It was a barren place, so to have your prey simply approach them in such a fashion did save the adventurer the trouble of looking for them...but location was an important factor to consider as well. There were no handrails at the edge of the path, just the snaking path itself and the endless ravine of empty space to either side. The adventurer would have no choice but to fight on that narrow space. Exhausting, if nothing else.

Typically, the fourth floor was a place only recommended for Silver-class adventurers and above—and this was one of the reasons.

There were many ways to deal with this situation, the methods often varying with party composition. A method that anyone could engage in was to run along the path as quickly as possible before the monsters appeared. They'd then be able to make it to the other side, and in doing so fight properly on solid ground without risk of falling. But due to the fact that I'd spent all this time staring at the scenery, this method was no longer available to me.

Chance factored heavily into the potential success of this option. Monsters could very well appear in the middle of that narrow path, and the party would then find themselves in a dire situation. It wasn't a method I could recommend.

What other methods could be employed, you might ask. The safest, and simplest, method was to attack from afar with magic. Since the winding stone path was an important part of the dungeon, it was deceptively strong, and it couldn't be damaged or destroyed by normal magic attacks. As such, it was possible to aim and fire long-range spells at the monsters as they ran along the path. If done well, an impact need not be fatal; it just had to knock the monster off-balance, causing it to fall into the bottomless space off the edges. In such a case, retrieval of materials would be regrettably impossible.

There were many more monsters on the floating mountain, though, so there was little to worry about in that regard.

This method was also effectively useless to me. I hadn't learned any long-range magic spells, and I couldn't even use offensive magic. All I had was my life magic.

Edel still seemed tired as well. He was sprawled out on my head, unmoving. It appeared he had no intentions of engaging in combat for quite some time. While I felt Edel should have had more stamina as my familiar... Well. That was probably the difference between master and familiar.

In light of all this, I had only one viable solution: a head-on clash with the monsters in question.

I'd proceed carefully along the path, taking care not to fall off, while at the same time striking and pushing my opponents into the void. If I were to fall for whatever reason, I'd have a good opportunity to test out my wings, though I couldn't be sure if they'd work. It'd be most preferable if I didn't fall at all...

Well, then, we should get going.

The monsters were already at the halfway mark of the stone path. There were three of them in total. It seemed the dungeon itself had a certain awareness about these things, only three as opposed to a horde. If you were to stay in this spot, unmoving, the amount of monsters advancing down the path would keep increasing. However, they most likely wouldn't keep coming if you advanced normally.

That said, I had no idea precisely how much time I had. It would serve me best to defeat the beasts quickly...

Although monsters of all kinds appeared on the fourth floor, the members of this specific "welcome party" were set in stone. These monsters walked on two legs, much like humans did, and their entire bodies were covered with shiny, glistening scales. In their jaws were rows of sharp teeth. Glittering eyes with long, vertical slits glared in my general direction. And they were armed with metallic equipment and weapons.

These creatures were none other than lizardmen.

In fact, lizardmen looked very similar to the wyvern-folk. The latter, however, were beastmen, and were simply a different type of sentient race, as opposed to monsters. But lizardmen were nothing more than another type of monster, and they would often attack any people they chanced upon.

As expected, the lizardmen began making a mad dash for me the very instant I set a single foot on the narrow path.

The monsters carried variety of weapons: swords, spears, and even shamshirs (curved hunting blades). While I momentarily wondered where they procured their weapons from, I quickly assumed that they behaved much like orcs did. In other words, said weapons were either stolen from fallen adventurers, or they appeared already equipped with them when reconstructed by the dungeon. The weapons weren't of very good material or make from the looks of it, though. If I had to guess, they were most likely armed with the latter. After all, adventurers who made it to the fourth floor were usually armed with somewhat respectable armaments.

Channeling mana into my body and blade, I braced myself, moving forward as I did so. Even then, I couldn't move toward them too quickly, lest the impact of our weapons launch me into the air. I deliberately placed one foot in front of the other.

The lizardmen didn't have similar concerns. They were running straight ahead, perhaps to gather enough momentum to push me into the depths upon contact. Considering that they were heavier than the typical adventurer, they may have assumed that such an impact wouldn't result in them losing their footing.

It would be most dangerous if we had any sort of bodily impact... But just then, a lizardman was already before me, swinging its weapon in a large horizontal arc. I quickly crouched, dodging the blow, and then sent a straight thrust into the monster's armored chest.

"Gigiii!!"

With a surprised, grating cry, the monster before me flew backward, only to slam straight into the very next charging lizardman. The lizardman in question was at least two times, if not three times as large as me. I could only assume it was that much heavier as well.

The last charging lizardman, unable to stop its attack, collided with the two before it. It promptly lost its footing and fell sideways down into the void. The lizardman's expression just before it fell somehow communicated great sorrow and regret, almost as if it were saying, "Ah, I've gone and done it now..."

"Gi! Gi...gigi..."

As it continued to fall into the abyss, its cries echoed, until it could no longer be heard. In the end, would that lizardman continue falling for eternity? Or would it eventually meet some sort of surface, only to be crushed by the impact? It was impossible to affirm from where I stood.

All I could think about was how I would like to avoid a similar fate. To that end...I'd have to ensure that the remaining two lizardmen went down as easily.

I turned my gaze to the two remaining monsters, now on their guard after witnessing the unfortunate death of their compatriot. They retreated slightly, placing some distance between us.

The lizardman behind the first crouched down low, as if to avoid any collateral damage should the one before it be sent flying back again. The one in front, in turn, adopted a defensive stance, lowering its center of gravity to prevent being launched again.

A somewhat troubling development, but I supposed that much was fine. I'd only decided to push one of them over the edge and into the abyss out of convenience. I could defeat the remaining two normally. I did require monster materials, and energy for Existential Evolution, so it was best to keep the remaining two on the surface.

As of late, I'd discovered that monsters around the level of a typical normal orc didn't provide very much, if any, life energy at all. I assumed monsters on the fourth floor would be able to provide me with what I needed.

On another note, I didn't feel the energy of the lizardman who fell off the edge flow into me. It was either still alive or disposed of in such a way that didn't release any energy at all.

I advanced slowly along the narrow path, intent on closing in on the two lizardmen before me.

Lizardmen in general were tall monsters, and they appeared somewhat larger as I approached. However, humans of such size weren't exactly a rarity. The monsters' large sizes didn't do them many favors when it came to precise maneuvers, either.

As I approached, the lizardman closest to me swung its weapon wildly, hoping to get a good attack in. I, however, moved faster than it did. Before it completed its swing, I'd already closed the distance between us and placed a good slash across its chest.

This was the fourth floor. Considering the relative hardness of a forest wolf's hide, I'd expected the skin of a lizardman to be even tougher and had infused my sword with even more mana as a result. But my blow merely grazed its flesh.

Hmph. Only a flesh wound...

As I continued my internal monologue, the lizardman before me retreated quickly. I supposed it had the upper hand when it came to brute strength. If I were to stray too close to it, the battle would become a simple comparison of strength, and I'd be at a disadvantage.

I deduced that a hit-and-run strategy, much like the one I'd employed just now, would be more effective in this particular case. If I'd used a Fusion Art with mana and spirit...I would've surely left a mark, if not a deep wound. Such a move, however, was resource-intensive. I had no way of knowing just how many strong enemies laid in wait beyond this path. For now, I had to conserve my strength.

In addition, while the blow I landed on the beast was but a scratch, it was by no means entirely harmless. I'd landed a well-placed slash, so a few more of these, and the lizardman would surely fall. As such, I could only justify using a Fusion Art if I was backed into a corner with no other choice.

I readied myself once more, adopting a combat stance as I approached the lizardman. The lizardman, on the other hand, changed its stance somewhat, withdrawing its arms and keeping them close to its body, as if to defend against similar attacks. Perhaps it was trying to prevent me from slashing its chest again.

But with its stance now altered, the lizardman had inadvertently shown me a weakness, an angle of attack. It was a defensive stance, yes, but not a perfect one. Due to the fact that its weapon was now close to its body, its reach and range drastically decreased. The only reason I'd approached the lizardman in the first place was due to its large size, so I was at a marked disadvantage when it came to attack range.

As such, I made a quick strike, closing the distance between us. Even if the monster were to abandon its advantage for the sake of defense, the battle would only swing in my favor.

I broke into a run and brought my blade down on the monster once more. As expected, the lizardman raised its own sword to guard against the blow, but its actions were significantly slower than before. Though, it did succeed in protecting its chest and torso region, and in doing so, had achieved its goal.

But the beast didn't expect me to follow up with a quick second strike to its face, and it couldn't defend itself in time.

"...Gigi!"

With a pained cry, the lizardman reared up, swinging its sword randomly in a mix of pain and fury. I disengaged in response, avoiding the blows.

Now at a safe distance, I looked at my foes once more. The lizardman with the injured face had stopped swinging and was currently glaring daggers at me. Drops of blue blood fell to the ground, giving rise to white streams of wispy smoke upon impact. Their blood was strongly acidic, I assumed. This would be one adversary I wouldn't be consuming...though I had quite some gluttonous tendencies myself.

The lizardman was now considerably hurt. Should I go in for the kill on my very next attack? I wasn't quite sure.

As I thought it over, the lizardman before me slowly stepped backward, exchanging positions with its comrade behind it.

Ah, yes. A logical move on their part.

This particular lizardman wielded a spear. A most troublesome foe, given the circumstances... Not a foe that I wanted to fight, but... Oh, but of course. I just didn't have to fight it then. That was a solution in and of itself.

With a well-practiced motion, I propelled myself forward, approaching the lizardman at a speed greater than any I had used in the current encounter. As expected, the spear-equipped lizardman thrust its weapon at me, to knock me off this narrow path. I parried its spear with the back of my blade, increasing my momentum as I continued running at the monster. I was now near its chest, but even then I didn't stop, instead neatly stepping to its side and running past the beast. It was a narrow path, yes, but there was enough space for the lizardmen to change positions with each other—and that meant there would be enough space for me.

With that singular motion, I was now behind the lizardman with the spear. Yet I continued running, making a beeline for the sword-equipped lizardman I'd injured earlier. I supposed the monster had intended to rest, or even spectate how I'd deal with its spear-wielding friend. But it could now only stare in surprise as I vaulted past its comrade. To think that lizardmen were capable of such expressions...

The injured lizardman was now visibly panicking.

But it was far too late. My sword was faster than its reactions.

I swung my blade horizontally, catching the monster straight in the torso and cleanly launching it off the narrow path. The impact of the blow had displaced the beast, and it sent the beast falling, eternally, into the bottomless abyss below.

Now was hardly the time to stop, however. I regained my momentum and continued running toward the floating mountain. I knew there was one more lizardman behind me, but it was impossible to continue fighting here. I wasn't too fond of fighting while constantly saddled with the fear of falling into the abyss.

I also wasn't very good with heights. While I did like some aspects, situations in which I could possibly fall were undoubtedly terrifying. This was why I continued sprinting forward, for the sake of reaching solid ground... All so I could reach that floating mountain, where I wouldn't have to fear the abyss again.

Turning around momentarily, my eyes met with those of the last lizardman, chasing after me. Its eyes were bloodshot, probably furious at the loss of its friends.

Well, then, perhaps it made more sense to not group up in a trio, and not run down such a dangerous, narrow path. But given the mysteries surrounding the general ecology of dungeons in general, it was impossible to guess their motives. Maybe they were forced to behave in a certain way by the dungeon—in this case, to mindlessly attack anyone that set foot onto the fourth floor. In fact, from what I understood, these three lizardmen always appeared so long as someone entered the area. To them, this may all be some sort of curse in and of itself.

Even so, I had no intention of going easy on the monster.

The lizardman stopped and faced me. Readying its weapon once more, it charged at me at full speed.

Up until a few moments ago, I would have been terrified at this prospect. Its weight, combined with the reach of its weapon, compounded my fears of falling into the abyss. But now that I was on solid ground, there was nothing to fear.

I ran straight at the monster as well, intent on meeting its charge head-on...only to step to the right at the last second. With a well-placed horizontal swing, my blade dug into its torso. Almost immediately, I followed through with a swing at its leg, and the lizardman momentarily lurched forward at the force of the blow.

This was the moment I'd been waiting for; its neck was now exposed. Channeling a significant amount of mana into my weapon, I brought my sword down upon its neck, pushing the weapon through skin, sinew, and bone. While my blade was met with quite a bit of resistance, it didn't last, and soon the lizardman's head fell.

It was a development very different from the hit-and-run encounters I'd had prior to this. I supposed not having much space to work with was significantly challenging to me. Yet another reminder that practice was required for such scenarios, so that I may fight at full capacity.

In any case, with this, I'd cleared the first notable obstacle of the fourth floor.

Gathering up what materials I could from the fallen lizardman, I stepped forward once more…

The floating mountain of the fourth floor was split into two main areas: a bare, somewhat rugged outer wall and a series of interconnected caves inside the mountain itself. The caves were as much a path as they were tunnels, and adventurers were often able to gather a variety of ores and stones from within.

That was my goal.

Given that I wanted to make and gift Alize with a light metal blade, the fourth floor was the perfect place to gather the required ores and metals.

I continued climbing up the floating mountain. Soon enough, I found an opening, and upon ascertaining that there were no monsters in the immediate vicinity, I carefully and quietly slipped into the cave.

The layout of the tunnels was somewhat complex. It was said that you could become lost, never to return, should you go too deep.

Under normal circumstances, a map of the complicated interior was required for navigation, and the typical adventurer would, of course, have to buy such an item. I, however, had the Map of Akasha. While it only displayed areas which I'd personally explored, there was now no possibility of me getting lost. Not having to purchase an additional map was also a bonus. In exchange, notes and points of interest typically shown on commercial maps were hidden from me, including areas where you could usually excavate for ore. I'd have to find all these locations myself.

As I continued walking along the tunnels, I caught sight of a partially collapsed wall. If I had to guess, someone before me had dug for ore in this very same spot. While some of these spots were marked with traces of excavation by others, most of them weren't. The possibility of ore yet remaining in this area was still high.

I withdrew a small, plank-like object from my magic bag. It was a cheap board of sorts, an item that reacted to faint traces of magic. It was a type of magic item in and of itself.

I raised it to the gap in the wall before me. After waiting for quite some time, I felt the board move ever so slightly as it gave off a faint glow. With this, I understood one thing: the ore I'd been looking for all this time was somewhere in these walls.

Specifically, I was looking for a type of metal known as "mana iron." It was much stronger than normal iron, and it also had a good affinity for mana in general. It was a relatively expensive metal.

Mana iron had some curious properties. If you were to channel mana through it, some of the mana would be absorbed by the metal, and the rest would be reflected and expelled.

It was this expulsion of mana that the board in my hands was reacting to. I'd surely find some mana iron if I were to dig further into this partially collapsed wall.

If I had Lorraine's level of skill, I'd be able to discern if objects had mana in them at a glance—but of course, such feats were beyond me.

Withdrawing a pickaxe from my bag, I turned to the wall, bracing myself.

Time to get what I came for.

The sharp clanging of metal on rock echoed throughout the tunnels as I continued mining the walls.

This particular pickaxe was made to tolerate mana. This allowed you to channel mana into it and continue excavating without any issues.

I persevered, digging myself deeper into the wall. If this were to take a long time, I'd most likely not have enough magic… But things should be fine at this pace.

I hope.

After a while, a faint glimmer beyond the rock walls caught my eye. It seemed to be a vein of some sort of ore—ore that contained the mana iron I was looking for.

I quickened my excavating pace. The ashen walls became noticeably harder as I continued digging, but with my now inhuman strength and the mana flowing through my veins, some slightly harder layers of rock were hardly a problem for me.

I was able to extract the ore I required surprisingly easily. However…

"The quality leaves much to be desired…"

I turned the piece of ore containing mana iron in my hands. Most of this ore piece consisted of impurities I didn't need, and a single glance was enough for me to tell.

If I were to use such a material, quite a large amount would have to be excavated for me to extract any sort of mana iron at all. And you would hardly be able to make a respectable weapon with ore of this quality. I wasn't looking to create some sort of artisanal weapon far exceeding normal standards, but this ore was simply... too impure for my purposes. While I could tolerate some impurities within metals in general, the quality of this vein was severely lacking.

I'd put a great deal of effort into excavating it, but nonetheless, I left it on the ground, intent on locating a better vein of ore.

I was hardly disappointed, however. In fact, I'd already anticipated this to a certain degree. It was said that ore in this floating mountain improved in purity and quality the deeper you went into the tunnels, so I'd already known to some extent that an excavation spot relatively near an entrance wouldn't provide me with many returns. I did want to excavate it in person, at least once, to affirm what I'd heard before moving on, though.

I supposed such was to be expected of a dungeon—you could never see what it had to offer without delving into its innermost depths.

I felt like I saw something flicker from the corner of my eye— a silhouette, or a shadow perhaps. Was someone else here? It wouldn't be strange for other adventurers to be present.

But...something was off about it. It was as if the existence of this being itself was...unstable. I couldn't say for sure.

In any case, I should have a look for myself…

But…no. It was precisely because of my curiosity that I had ended up with such a body in the first place. I should be placing my safety before all else…

At least, that was what I thought. Soon enough, though, I gave in to my curiosity. If I didn't have such a personality, I wouldn't have had to go through all that I had up till now. But I supposed me acting this way was very much a given.

All I had to do was immediately escape should there be any sign of danger. Considering the amount of energy I'd expended thus far, I could safely say I could escape at a reasonable speed.

But of course, it'd be most trying should I run into some sort of dragon again. Though that was a one-off case of bad luck. I assumed such a thing wouldn't happen again.

I approached the place where I'd seen the shadow.

But…

There was no one there. Perhaps it was just my imagination…

"…Who are you? Where did you come from?" a voice said from behind me.

Shocked, I immediately turned around, only to see a young girl standing before me.

She was…very young. Perhaps about five or six years of age. But the aura she had about her was anything but childish. Her gaze was full of suspicion, even irritation. It was an expression only adults could muster.

I was at a loss for what to say, my mouth gaping as I struggled to find the words. Just as I did…

"…I don't know. No… I… I am…"

Another voice from behind me. Not one that manifested from my throat.

There was another person there, so I turned around—only to come face-to-face with a strange individual, dressed in a tattered and ragged old robe.

The robed individual didn't seem very normal at all. Gazing upon him, I couldn't help but feel that he was an unknown existence I could never understand, and my heart was filled with a great sense of unease. It seemed the individual was thinking, lost in thought at the girl's question.

Just who is this person...

As that thought entered my mind, the young girl stepped right through me, continuing to speak to the robed individual. Now that I was observing her from a distance, I could see that the girl was somewhat...translucent.

Did she even really exist? Or was she simply not physically here? Was that why she could not see me?

Upon closer inspection, the robed individual seemed slightly translucent as well.

"You don't know? You don't know where you came from? But to come here, you must have come from somewhere else...and yet, you don't know?" the girl asked.

The robed individual shook his head. "I... I don't know. I don't know. I don't know...anything. I... I am. What am I? Where is this?!"

As they shouted, their shaking intensified. Soon after, the hood on their head was shaken clean off.

...Hey, now.

I wasn't expecting to see anything quite like it. I felt a deep sense of surprise rising up from within.

The robed individual standing before me...was a skeleton. A skeleton with a faint light in its eye sockets... A skeleton with logic, and the capability to reason. There looked to be a complicated tattoo across its skull, the pattern glowing a faint blue.

I'd never seen such a tattoo before… But this was unmistakably… a skeleton.

A skeleton—a monster much like what I used to be, quite a while ago.

…*Who was that,* I wondered.

With a single step, I approached the two. I wanted to see this strange robed skeleton up close.

Unfortunately, as if sensing my intent, the robed individual slowly dissipated, fading out of existence, before vanishing into thin air altogether. The girl questioning him vanished too, her image slowly losing its color before fading into nothingness. All that was left in the barren tunnels were myself and the silent rock faces surrounding me. It was a most lonely feeling, as if what had just occurred before me was nothing more than an illusion.

"What was that all about…?" I said despite myself.

No one answered my query. The only response was an empty echo, softly reverberating through the tunnels.

Were occurrences like this common on the fourth floor?

No… That couldn't possibly be true. If that really were the case, there would have been a flood of rumors about it in the taverns by now. At the very least, I should have heard about it, one way or another.

Then…could it be possible that this strange phenomenon only occurred because of who I was?

Why would that be the case…? Was it just a coincidence? Or was this something that simply had to happen?

I had no way of knowing.

After pondering the issue for a while, I gave up, realizing that I simply didn't have any answers. I supposed I could think about it another time.

There were many inexplicable things in the world—unsolved mysteries, including the reason for me becoming an undead. It was important to discern between what you could know, and what you might never know. It was an important survival skill in its own right.

For now, I had to focus on what I needed to do: material gathering.

The deeper I went into the tunnels, the higher the purity and quality of the mana iron I sought. And so…I must continue moving forward. As for what had happened today, I supposed I could just tuck it away in some corner of my heart, for now.

"Guuugyaaa!!!"

A cry most inhuman rang out through the tunnels.

My sword was currently buried in the face of the monster before me—the face of a mina goblin. I'd been aiming for its neck, but the monster was more agile than I'd expected, and it ended up dodging the blow.

As their name suggested, mina goblins were different from the common goblin. For starters, they lived in places abundant with ore, commonly mountains and the like. They also possessed certain unique skills, namely, that of smelting. Although they were hardly as skilled as the dwarves, and weren't capable of creating precise instruments and magic items, they knew enough about smelting to create swords, shields, and the like.

This meant there should be a smelting chamber somewhere in this mountain, though I had no idea as to where exactly such a place could be. While adventurers had successfully located and destroyed said smelting chambers repeatedly in the past, another one would eventually pop up in its place.

Infrastructure on such a scale didn't seem like an easy undertaking… But then again, the dungeon was a huge place. If you were serious about exploring the entirety of the fourth floor, you would definitely need more than one or two days. A few weeks, perhaps, or maybe even a few months.

Even so, it might still be impossible for you to see everything it had to offer. Given the sheer size of the floor, it was very possible that several of these chambers were partially constructed, and should one ever be destroyed, the goblins in question would simply move on to the next one. All that had to be done was to transport some specialized items from one location to another, and that was that. If this were indeed true, these chambers would never be completely destroyed, no matter how much time came to pass.

At the very least, mina goblins were capable of constructing simple magic items, and they were also able to prevent the heat and smoke from these chambers from giving away their location. This made finding such a chamber difficult. *If these goblins were armed with such knowledge, why not simply live at peace with humans,* you might think, and in reality, certain groups of goblins did live this way.

The mina goblins on the fourth floor, however, appeared to have some sort of pride that man couldn't possibly hope to understand. Perhaps this was the reason why they couldn't be at peace with humanity in general.

As a result of all their smelting and crafting, mina goblins looked different than the average goblin and were often armed with reasonably well-made armor and weaponry. Even the color of their skin was different; a sort of natural adaptation to their rocky habitat, perhaps. The skin of a mina goblin was earth-brown, compared to the green skin of a normal goblin. They were also significantly more muscular, probably due to all the ore they excavated in their free time.

If normal goblins were small and annoying ankle-biters, mina goblins were very much like miniature yet muscular gorillas.

Truly horrifying.

The speed of their swings, compounded by their sheer muscular power, meant that mina goblins were much more formidable foes than lizardmen. They were also trained to handle weaponry, and they had a certain amount of martial prowess to their movements.

Although it sustained a wound from my blade, the goblin soon snapped out of its panic, immediately calming down and staring threateningly in my direction. As expected, monsters became increasingly more difficult to slay as you ventured into the deeper floors...

It occurred to me that staying here for a while and absorbing the life force of these monsters wouldn't be all that bad an idea. I didn't mean to say that I hadn't become stronger, but perhaps the pace of my descent was a little too fast. I should have gauged my own capabilities before deciding to go all the way down to the fourth floor, but it was a little too late for such thoughts.

Despite that, I hadn't sustained any grievous injuries, and I was still managing to fight my foes on relatively equal, albeit strained, footing. Things would indeed be bad if I'd decided to go any deeper.

Or perhaps I should fight at that level of difficulty, and maybe reach new heights of growth by continually exposing myself to danger...? *No, no. That would be far too reckless.*

In any case, those were thoughts better attended to at home. For now, it was more important to deal with the mina goblin before me.

It was holding a large, two-handed axe in its hands, a weapon I'd find difficult to control, much less swing about. To the mina goblin, however, the axe likely didn't weigh very much at all.

The weapon was crude; not only was it heavy, it was also difficult to control... Yet the mina goblin seemed to have mastered it ages ago. It blocked my swings with the flat side of its axe, turning its two-handed weapon into a makeshift shield. As my blade deflected off its surface, it would immediately counterattack.

"...Kuh!"

I'd dodged a swing from the monster by a hair, yet the mina goblin didn't let up on its attacks. It held its axe firmly, swinging it down as if to split me into two clean halves. While I was unsure if my body as it was right now would be easily split apart in the first place, I wasn't too keen to find out first-hand.

It suddenly dawned on me that death could come knocking at my door at any instance.

In a slight panic, I dodged as best as I could, eager to avoid the descending two-handed axe. My evasion wasn't perfect, however, and the blade of the weapon grazed my cheek. A fine line traced across my features...before healing up in seconds, disappearing altogether.

It appeared that I now had the ability to recover from simple cuts relatively quickly.

I did feel a slight sense of fatigue from that, though. I could heal myself, yes, but there were tangible risks involved in the process. After all, adventurers who had actually faced vampires did affirm that they often healed up immediately after suffering most slashing wounds.

While lesser vampires also possessed these regenerative qualities, the spike of fatigue I just felt may very well indicate that there was a limit to my regeneration…especially if I got terribly injured. I supposed even vampires couldn't regenerate indefinitely…

While I didn't know of anyone who'd conducted tests to affirm this, nor were there records to that effect, most individuals who chose to fight vampires often decided to go straight for their weak points. In such a case, regenerative limits didn't really matter. After all, no one would go out of their way to slay a vampire with a more roundabout method.

Although my wound was light, the impact of the blow was significant, and I rolled for some distance before recovering, once again raising my blade toward the mina goblin. Affirming that I was about to launch an attack, the mina goblin raised the flat side of its axe once more, as if to defend—

"…Gyaaaahh!" the mina goblin cried out as it swung its axe backward instead.

What…? I thought to get a closer look, and there was Edel. My familiar had launched a spell at the beast: Wind Blade. By the time the goblin swung its axe around, however, Edel was already at a safe distance, much to my relief.

With the goblin now sufficiently distracted, I seized the opportunity, dashing forward and swinging my blade at its exposed head. My weapon cut deep, fracturing its skull, before splitting the goblin into two clean halves.

With a shudder, the mina goblin fell to the ground, fresh blood spewing forth from the separated corpse.

Although I proceeded with the dissection of the mina goblin, it soon became evident that there wasn't very much to recover from it. Its weapons and equipment, along with the magic crystal near its heart, were useful, but there was no tangible use for the rest of the carcass.

I supposed I could remove its right ear and take it with me as a bounty, but there were currently no active hunting requests at the guild. Since I didn't even remember seeing such a request in the first place, it was most likely a pointless venture—but I decided to take the ear anyway. A single ear wouldn't take up much space.

As for its weapons and equipment... Well, while they were indeed smithed with mana iron excavated from these tunnels, goblin blacksmithing techniques weren't all that impressive. The purity of the ore and the construction of the weapon left much to be desired. The axe was also a goblin-sized, so it wouldn't be of much value even if I did take it with me.

I guess it was technically possible to melt the axe down and re-use the metal itself, but that would require putting more time and resources into the refinement process. At the end of the day, it seemed cheaper to simply bring any blacksmith a piece of ore containing mana iron instead.

I decided to leave the axe where it lay.

The magic crystal, however, was of a fair size and quality. I promptly decided to take it with me. The crystal could be used as material for the wands…and if that wasn't possible, it could always be sold for some coin.

…I supposed this was all you could hope to extract from the carcass of a mina goblin.

With that, I set out, starting my journey through the caves once more.

I felt like I'd ventured deep into these tunnels. I could feel the air stagnating around me as I continued on.

Given how the tunnels were, it wasn't entirely impossible for certain sections to be filled with poisonous gas. While the concentration of these gases wasn't high, I'd heard of certain tunnels occasionally becoming sealed off due to a sudden increase in gas concentrations. There were no such warnings from the guild now, however. Even so, I couldn't be entirely sure that there weren't any noxious gasses somewhere.

Basically, it was safe to assume that the surroundings were poisonous to a certain degree.

But I was particularly resistant to such poisons. During my time as a ghoul, I had been completely immune to all sorts of poisons. I assumed it had been the same during my time as a skeleton.

Even though I'd since evolved into a lesser vampire, my resistance hadn't seemed to fade. It was times like these when I felt grateful for this body of mine. I was able to progress without issues.

It hardly felt like I was omnipotent or immortal though— the fact that my regeneration seemed to have a limit reminded me of that fact. Perhaps I'd been somewhat reckless as of late, thinking it was fine to do certain, usually fatal things, disregarding the danger simply because I was an undead. Maybe I just wasn't very receptive to danger... No, if I had to describe it, it'd be more of a feeling— a feeling that this wasn't enough to kill me.

An overconfidence in my abilities, perhaps. Or maybe a condition brought about by my status as a member of the walking dead. Regardless, this case in particular seemed more of the former, so I slowed down, proceeding cautiously as I checked my surroundings. It was cowardly adventurers who often lived the longest—so goes the saying.

Eventually, a large set of doors appeared before my eyes.

Well, now...how should we go about doing this?

Or rather, what should we do in the first place? This set of doors was obviously an entrance to a boss room. Would it be all right to simply step inside?

My undead intuition was egging me on. *We should go. Let's go inside already,* it said. My old adventurer's sense, however, was begging me to stop, reasoning that I should slay some more monsters in this area before attempting such a thing. It was undoubtedly the safer option.

But...it couldn't be too bad.

Well, then...we should get going.

If there was any danger, all we had to do was run. Return to this place.

It was a boss room, yes, but since it was on the fourth floor, I highly doubted it could be an inescapable chamber. Under normal circumstances, said chambers were only found at around 40 floors deep. Considering the chamber I encountered in the Water Moon Dungeon, though, I supposed I couldn't declare that as an ironclad fact... But even so, that was more the exception than the norm.

And unlike the previous occurrence, I hadn't entered some secret passage, gotten teleported somewhere, then overcome a series of obstacles to arrive at this door. No—this door simply stood here, plainly announcing its presence. If there really was some complicated mechanism to this whole thing, it would have at least been discussed by the adventurers who frequented this floor often.

All this in mind, I concluded that this was hardly a special room. It simply couldn't be the case...and so, it should be fine to enter.

I repeated this to myself, over and over again, as I placed a hand on the door.

Was I being careless? Reckless? Or was I simply uneasy? And yet...somehow I had a feeling that this particular boss room wouldn't pose much of a threat.

At the very least...I could escape from it anytime.

I did feel that something was off though. My so-called undead intuition perhaps?

Though, irregular and strange things could happen to an adventurer from time to time. If I got too caught up in the specifics and continuously hesitated, I'd never get anywhere.

So...I supposed this was all right. I wasn't wrong; I wasn't being reckless.

I gave the doors a good push and looked on silently as they swung open with a low rumble.

Ah. It seemed it was a normal boss room after all.

As I peaked through the door, it looked like my deductions were largely accurate.

There was, however, a bit of a problem with the boss monster perched in the middle of the room. Huge body, glistening scales, four legs, and a large horn of ore and rock on its head... All meant to showcase its strength. A single look was enough to suggest that it was by no means a weak foe—the monster before me was a terra drake.

It was a lesser dragon of sorts, more accurately a subspecies that commonly preferred to live underground. But even though it was a lesser subspecies, it was still a dragon. Relatively speaking, it was a monster of significant strength. It wasn't normally associated with appearing on the fourth floor, but the possibility of it doing so was evident.

In any case, the terra drake in the center of the room wasn't very big. It might be large compared to me, but if I were to compare it to a mature dragon, it was somewhat smaller—about 25% of a mature specimen's size. If I had to guess...probably around four meters. If this were the case...then perhaps I could do something about this drake.

Even so...I couldn't help but feel that its size was strange. Normally, dragons of all types grew larger and gained strength as they aged. Given that this drake was somewhat smaller than a mature dragon, I supposed it wasn't overwhelmingly powerful.

Basically, I gave the matter serious thought as I sized the terra drake up.

Then I glanced at the door. It wasn't thick by any means. I could certainly break through and escape if it came down to it.

That in mind, I could reasonably assume that this wasn't a boss room of the inescapable variety. Of course, there was the possibility that the door was made of some sort of special material, making it difficult to destroy, but it didn't seem all that different from the rock walls around it.

Perhaps it was a little silly to think about escaping before the fight had even started, but this, too, was an important strategy to consider. If these were the factors at hand, then…very well.

Gathering my thoughts, I slowly entered the room. The door showed no signs of closing even as I approached the center of the chamber. Escape from this encounter was possible, as I had expected.

This development filled me with a deep sense of relief. Slowly, I drew my sword and began channeling mana into its blade.

A combat stance.

The four-legged terra drake didn't move an inch. It merely continued staring in my general direction. Perhaps it was simply observing me or waiting for me to get closer. Whatever the case, this meant I should strike first…or so I thought.

Slowly, I accelerated, breaking into a run. In the midst of my sprint…

"…GUURRRGGYYYAAAAAA!!!"

An ear splitting roar arose from its throat.

But that wouldn't stop me. Without any hesitation, I aimed for the head of the beast, swinging my blade as I closed in. Unfortunately…

Tink!

With a metallic clash, my blade was blocked. The terra drake had defended against my attack.

This wasn't because of its hard scales. Given that terra drakes were a subspecies of lesser dragon, you would expect their skin and scales to be impressively tough. I had already known that before my attack.

While it was also true that I'd never properly fought a terra drake before now, I did, at the very least, have some knowledge about the creature, including knowledge of its natural defenses. That was exactly why I'd channeled more mana into my weapon and body than I ever had before .

Despite this, the monster had been able to defend against my blow. As I brought down my sword, what appeared to be a shield of rock and stone had risen up around the terra drake's head. It was a helmet-like shield, made from the stone and rock scattered in the nearby area, most likely spontaneously crafted as soon as I swung my blade.

This was none other than magic, and used by monsters at that.

More precisely, it was elemental magic. Compared to the magic that humans wielded today, elemental magic was very old. However, its usefulness and power shouldn't be underestimated. While incantations and the like were useful when it came to magic, a visual image of the spell itself was important as well. Elemental magic, on the other hand, drew on natural phenomena. As such, it was very easy to visualize.

In addition, there were other ways elemental magic could be utilized advantageously, and I had just witnessed one of them. The ability to use your surroundings as weapons. For example, if earth elemental magic was used in a place where there was an abundance of rock and soil, it would be simple to gather and extract it from the surroundings. The amount of magic required to do this would also be reduced, so it would be possible for you to increase the destructive power of the spell or even enhance your magic. This was exactly what the terra drake before me had done. It had gathered stones and rocks from its surroundings, and had used them to form a shield to defend against my attacks.

Given the nature of the terrain around me, I assumed that the rocks it was using contained veins of mana iron, and in high concentrations. These rocks, in turn, were further strengthened by the terra drake's magic and formed a formidable defense.

I had no concrete proof of all this, of course, but it remained unchanged that the drake successfully defended against my attack. If you were to think about it normally, rationally, this would be the endgame.

I'd launched a surprise maneuver, one infused with high amounts of mana. One of the strongest attacks in my arsenal, and yet…the drake defended itself so easily. But if I were to give up here, I'd never become a Mithril-class adventurer, no matter how much time I put into it.

I still had many moves left, though. I kept my ace up my sleeve. Plus, that rock shield may yet have some sort of undiscovered weakness.

I momentarily retreated, instead intending to observe the monster's next move. The terra drake, as if reading my mind, charged at me in response, closing in at a fearsome speed.

Just as I realized how bad the situation was, I found the drake already before me. Panicking, I dodged to the side desperately. Its response was swift. Pivoting its giant body, it spun, swinging its tail sideways and down. Just as I thought I'd dodged the blow, in came its tail, hardly giving me any breathing room. The only thing I could do was raise the flat of my blade. The drake's tail made contact, and I was sent sailing through the air.

Wham!

I slammed into one of the chamber's walls with a resounding thud. I could hear pieces of fragmented rock raining around me. Such was the force of the impact, the power of the blow.

But the terra drake was far from done. It pressed the attack, charging directly at me.

I must avoid another hit…

That was the singular thought that filled my mind as I felt the previous impact radiate through me.

If I dodged to the side again, I'd just receive yet another hit from its tail. In that case…

I remained still, allowing the drake to continue its charge. I was aiming for a specific moment, my foot braced against the wall, just before it hit me.

My goal was the terra drake's back.

Could I really do this…?

It was like the very flow of time itself stretched out—each moment felt like an eternity. I was in a most vulnerable state.

If it came to it, I could infuse spirit into my wings and quickly launch myself away. But the drake would surely give chase again if I did so.

Please…work.

Slowly but surely, the grains of time crawled on.

The head was now close enough… I pushed off from the wall, aiming for its surface. The monster still hadn't noticed.

The drake made contact with where I'd been moments ago, kicking up a large cloud of dust, impairing its vision.

I, on the other hand, didn't have a normal sense of sight. Instead, I could see as most undead did: via body warmth.

Thank you, oh body of mine.

In fact, being able to shrug off being slammed into a rock wall with only light dizziness and vertigo was in no small part due to this body. Under normal circumstances, I would have definitely died.

I stepped down, my foot now unmistakably on the terra drake's head. I'd already raised my sword, its blade descending upon the beast.

If the drake noticed me, I'd be vulnerable and exposed to a counterattack. However, this was also my single, greatest chance. If the attack connected, I'd be able to fell the terra drake with a single blow.

That was my intention as I brought my sword down.

My blade pierced its neck. A little more and I'd have it, but...

Almost instantly, it formed a rock shield around its neck, knocking my blade away. It seemed I wouldn't be able to finish it so easily, though I did leave behind a considerable wound.

It was now evident that the shield wasn't impervious to attacks. Unfortunately, it was equally evident that such an attack would no longer work on the drake.

I ran swiftly down the monster's back, intending to escape from its field of vision. Even a terra drake couldn't accurately pinpoint the location of a foe on its back. As if understanding this, the drake began thrashing about, trying to dislodge me.

I presumed that it was about to start spinning in place again, but by this point, I was already firmly on the ground. Landing by the drake's side, I could now see its underbelly.

It's now or never.

I liberally channeled both mana and spirit into my weapon. It was time... The Mana-Spirit Fusion Art.

Swinging my weapon in a large horizontal arc, I slashed it across the drake's exposed belly. Unlike the hard scales around its neck and back, the skin of a terra drake's stomach was considerably softer and easier to slice into. There was, of course, the fact that I was using a Fusion Art, but I hadn't anticipated such little resistance. This must be the monster's weak point.

This, too, was written in the monster codex I'd read. However, it was extremely difficult to get the drake to show its belly to an enemy, making it a difficult area to hit. I was lucky this time.

The terra drake had a surprising amount of vitality. It refused to die even with its belly sliced open. Almost immediately, it stood up once more and headed in my direction. With a few stomps of its feet, spears of rock and earth arose from the ground, one after another. I dodged the earthen spears one by one, closing the distance between us to finish the job. The monster, seeing my approach, intensified its attacks. Spears of earth and stone now formed in mid-air and rapidly hurtled toward me.

Perhaps it was due to its injuries, but the drake seemed distracted, and its magical attacks were anything but accurate. Even so, the attacks were still impressive in terms of impact. They weren't much of a threat, however, compared to the drake's behavior before.

I arrived at the front of the monster and jumped up high, aiming for its head. I assumed the rock shield would appear right about now...and as expected, it did just that.

As I brought my sword down, the terra drake attempted to put up its shield once more. The integrity of the gathered rocks, however, had decreased drastically. Loosely-gathered rocks were nothing more than soft flesh before the force of my Mana-Spirit Fusion Art.

With a single, smooth motion, the blade of my weapon sliced cleanly through the terra drake's neck, and its head fell. Almost at the same time, its body went limp and collapsed onto the ground with a loud, booming thud.

The entire body of a terra drake made for good materials, not to mention its magic crystal, too. Scales, teeth, claws, eyes... All these parts were useful, high-quality materials. Considering the capacity of my magic bag, it was extremely regrettable that I couldn't transport the entire carcass back.

Realistically speaking, it was sufficient to simply gather the magic crystal, scales, fangs, claws, and eyes. It was as if I were picking out parts to eat.

Ahh, if only I had a larger magic bag... Perhaps one would show up at an auction soon? I couldn't purchase such a bag at a run-of-the-mill store. There was the issue of price as well...though I could simply sell the rest of the tarasque to cover the expense.

In any case, procuring a considerably large bag might be quite difficult. Even if I did, I wouldn't get rid of my old one. In fact, having two at my disposal would make transporting materials that much easier.

After some time, I finished dissecting the terra drake. It was now time to move on. I was considerably tired, however, and it occurred to me that I should return as soon as possible. I had enough magic crystals at this point. But I had yet to excavate a suitable vein of mana iron.

I guess I could press on...just a little longer.

This mentality of mine was perhaps a little too reckless...

There were two doors in the chamber that had once housed the terra drake. I'd entered from one of those doors, so the other was presumably the exit. It had remained closed all throughout the battle, but it swung open as soon as the terra drake was defeated.

This must be the way forward.

As I approached the door, I was surprised at what I saw beyond. There were no obvious paths, but instead a steep edge terminating much like a cliff. I could see small footholds and grips, means of descending this sheer surface.

While I wasn't facing a mountain, judging from the darkness that lay before me, and the fact that I was surrounded by a sea of stone, I could tell where I was.

It was a large hole in the ground; a cavernous depression. It was wide, perhaps stretching on for at least a kilometer in each cardinal direction. The ceiling was high as well.

Although the surroundings were dark and visibility was poor, I could say with certainty that this place differed greatly from the tunnels that I'd passed through up until this point. In addition, there was a lot of equipment—magic items perhaps—simply lying about. It reminded me of a mine. There were even tracks and mining carts. From the looks of it, this appeared to be a man-made space.

This was, however, a location in the dungeon. It was all but impossible for humans to simply create a mine here, so it was safe to assume that this, too, was something created by the dungeon's mysterious devices.

There were occasionally tales of places within dungeons that contained towns, cities, castles—impossible sights that couldn't possibly have been crafted by the hands of men. A place like this wasn't all that mysterious. The only mystery was the very existence of the dungeon itself. If anything, odd features on the various floors, such as this one, were considerably more normal.

It was still fair to say that this strange sight caught my attention, though. When the dungeons were created, were references made to parts of human civilization? Given that castles and towns could be found within them, my assumptions most likely had some degree of truth.

Normally, dungeons featured forests, caves, and other natural landscapes, but human settlements were somewhat natural occurrences as well. If you thought about it that way, the sight before me wasn't all that strange.

Then there was the fact that dungeons continued creating monsters, no matter how much time went by. That by itself was an astonishing display of creative force.

Regardless of why this space was formed, the fact that I was now standing in it did not change.

This was a mine. A place for excavation. I had come here in search of high-quality mana iron, so…this was the place to do so.

I slowly descended the cliff, sticking close to the wall. Eventually I reached the bottom, and I began observing my surroundings. I couldn't see very far due to the lack of light, but I recalled seeing the moving silhouettes of some monsters from my observations at the top of this pit. There were no silhouettes near where I landed though, so I was able to descend without too much worry.

After some time, it became clear that there were no monsters in my immediate vicinity. A bit of relief for the weary adventurer. There were instead more mining carts, and what appeared to be a magic item of some sort, as well as a switch-like object.

Hmm… What should I do?

Would anything happen if I pressed that switch? The safest thing to do would be to not touch it at all…but that would be a most boring development. Safety took precedence over my boredom, of course, but…there didn't appear to be any traps, or danger, in the immediate area. I'd also come from above, so it wasn't like anything would fall from the ceiling. And I wasn't standing on a pitfall trap...

If I was going to press the switch, then maybe I should just get it over with. If anything untoward happened upon its activation, I could simply turn it off again.

...Well. I couldn't discount the fact that I may not be able to turn the switch off, but...

Whatever the case... *Click.*

With a soft, mechanical sound, the switch depressed under the weight of my finger, and almost immediately, the darkness was illuminated by light. Instinctively, I looked up. The light source was very high up indeed, its rays shining down into this massive pit.

In other words...this was a light switch for the mine's lights.

...I was just glad it wasn't a trap.

The lights didn't illuminate the entire space, but instead lit up my surroundings, up to a few tens of meters. I assumed there were other switches like this one in the darkness, and the rest of the pit would remain dark unless they were pressed.

I, of course, could see in the darkness to some degree. My much-vaunted Undead Sight was mainly used to track living creatures, however, so it didn't help much for inanimate objects like switches. While I couldn't say being a vampire was completely without benefits, it just so happened that my vampiric abilities weren't very useful in this situation.

All I had to do was find some rocks containing veins of mana iron, then excavate it. But to do so, I needed a normal light source. I supposed there was no other way but to dig, find a switch, and repeat ad infinitum.

As I stood contemplating the situation, I noticed the presence of monsters close by. Observing quietly, I saw the silhouettes of what appeared to be two mina goblins slowly approaching the illuminated space. The lights were turned on, so someone or something must be here...was probably what the goblins thought.

So, this was a trap of some sort after all...?

This meant that illuminating other areas would draw monsters to them in a similar fashion, though I couldn't be absolutely sure.

In any case, I needed to deal with these two mina goblins before inspecting my surroundings for ore. I'd seen some promisingly-colored walls when I'd inspected the pit from above. All I had to do was find them, excavate the mana iron, and that...was that.

Or so I thought...

Clink! Clank!

The sound of my pickaxe hitting rock echoed through the air. I'd already disposed of the two mina goblins that had wandered into the light earlier. They were formidable foes, but they didn't have any companions. After I slew the two of them, no other mina goblins showed up. It seemed camaraderie wasn't a goblin's strong point.

With that done, I circled around the pit, following the curved walls, striking at any parts that looked promising. I did, for the record, look for the appropriate switch, and I managed to illuminate the area I was currently working in.

It seemed like someone had been here before me, as there were traces of excavation in this particular wall, and I could see veins of metal shining through. Surely I'd be able to gather high-quality mana iron here.

Honestly speaking, even the rocks at my feet that had crumbled off the wall were of a respectable quality. I could tell just by picking one up and staring at it.

In that case…

Of course, if I was going to dig for ore, a piece from the ground wouldn't do. I intended to go from vein to vein, searching for the perfect place, then excavate a great amount and bring that all back home.

For now though…this was enough. I left that vein behind, and headed toward yet another possible excavation point…

The feeling of fear and apprehension began to settle in only after the third excavation point I'd visited. By then, I was all filled up and ready to return… It was then that it happened.

I'd been observing and walking along the walls of this strange pit, finally beginning to understand the structural intricacies of this place. The ground I was walking on and excavating from was actually on top of another space—another floor, I surmised. I somehow felt that this other floor beneath me existed.

Perhaps it was because my surroundings were too dark, and that's why I didn't notice. I didn't know that there may be something lurking in this space beneath my feet.

I suddenly had a feeling—a feeling that something was there. It just so happened that the light shining on the third excavation spot illuminated this cavernous space below, so I slowly approached, carefully hugging the cliff walls as I peered down.

It was then that I saw it—a terrifying monster.

I thought that the faint rays of light shining through the cracks had already hit the ground of the next floor. Then the ground itself began moving, ever so slowly.

My eyes and Undead Sight could see creatures in the darkness. This much was true. However, there were exceptions. For instance, your abilities may fail to activate when faced with an incredibly strong foe. For the first time in my life, I experienced this firsthand.

What, exactly, was this thing lurking in the darkness? The dim lighting made it hard to discern.

The first thing I understood was that the ground I'd seen, a carpet of smooth, shining rock, was nothing more than a part of a larger creature. Its skin, or hide, seemed to continue on indefinitely. Then, ever so slightly, the light shining from above illuminated what appeared to be the creature's face, just for a split second.

An eye. An eye as large as my entire person.

At this point, I was still unsure. Should I escape? It looked like the creature's eye was currently closed; it appeared to be asleep. I could see that much, even at this distance.

I felt a wave of terror wash over me. I could never, under any circumstances, challenge this monster, not even with my current abilities.

I couldn't let the monster notice me, couldn't let it become aware of my presence. Instinctively, I felt a strong pull; I had to leave this place as soon as possible.

For some reason, during my journey down to the fourth floor, I'd felt that I could keep advancing. So long as I was cautious, I wouldn't be exposed to any potentially fatal dangers.

Before my journey, I'd read up on the different types of monsters and their strengths, the various traps, and all sorts of other dangers present. My assumption that I could keep pressing on was nothing more than an internal rationalization.

However, what lay beneath me now... I didn't have to assume or rationalize anything. A single look was enough to tell me that this foe, this existence, was beyond me.

What lay beneath me was none other than an earth dragon. It had an almost frog-like, bearded face, with eyes that betrayed intelligence and logic. On its back were two tiny wings, seemingly out of place with the rest of its huge body.

Its size, however, was anything but frog-like. Forty...? No. Fifty meters perhaps...? It was huge. Massive. Entire towns and cities would crumble to dust should it thrash around with its giant body. Buildings wouldn't even last a single second. There were even quite a few legends of angered earth dragons flattening entire villages, towns, and even kingdoms and countries.

It did much more than just thrash about. With it's sheer size and power, it could easily cause earthquakes. The earth would ripple and shake, buildings would crumble, streets would be swallowed and destroyed. Stones falling from the sky would make short work of any who attempted escape, and those lucky enough to get out would become feed for its minions.

To think something like that laid here...

There were no reports. Nothing at all.

Why? How? Something so large... There was no way no one knew about this.

As I continued thinking, observing the earth dragon from a distance, its previously closed eye suddenly opened. With a deafeningly loud rumble, the dragon stood and began moving.

This was bad... Had I been found out? I see... So my life would end here and now.

A familiar feeling assaulted my body. It was what I'd felt when I first encountered a "dragon." A feeling close to surrender, yet much akin to release…along with the sheer emotional force of seeing a legendary creature up close.

It was a relatively rare thing to experience. You would simply think it was all right to die right there, and a part of me felt that way as well.

This may be a given, but I couldn't simply die in a place like this. I was going to become a Mithril-class adventurer. That was why I hadn't given up, even after my body became like this.

However…what, exactly, was I to do in such a situation? All it took was a single swipe of the earth dragon's massive limbs and I'd surely give up the ghost then and there.

There was an impossibly large gap between us, one that couldn't be compensated for just because I was an undead.

I… I couldn't do anything. Not one single thing. Not anything at all.

That gigantic life form apparently hadn't noticed me yet. Perhaps it already knew of my presence but felt I wasn't worth the effort. All I could do was pray that this was the case.

I suddenly realized I could hear my own heartbeat. My own heartbeat, in this lifeless body of mine. I felt a cold sweat come over me, my muscles slowly cramping up. I was shivering, but I did my best to stifle all sound, my life depending on it.

Then—

For a single instant, I felt our eyes meet.

Or…maybe it was just my imagination.

Slowly, the earth dragon turned around, and with its great limbs, began digging—deeper and deeper. Its massive body began fading into the ground.

Consider the fact that we were in the middle of a large, floating mountain. The so-called ground here was in fact hard, solid bedrock.

Not that this mattered to the earth dragon. It simply continued to casually dig.

As expected of an earth dragon.

All I could do was stand there, taking the utmost care not to make a sound, doing all I could to hide my presence.

The dragon's digging dislodged a small rain of rocks and debris. I, in turn, had to dodge, deploy a shield spell… There was quite a bit for me to do. The dislodged rocks weren't even a type of attack, merely a side effect of the earth dragon's subterranean movement. However, each individual rock had as much force as the terra drake's stone spears… It was truly terrifying.

Surely, a Mithril-class adventurer would be able to fight something like this head-on. I suddenly became very aware of just how far away from my goal I was.

One day, I would surely defeat this monster.

One day… I thought, deeply and solemnly.

I…see.

I was staring at where the earth dragon had once been. It was now a place dominated by loneliness, not a single trace of the sheer strength and power that had been present there just moments ago. I stared out at the now-empty space. Although the earth dragon had just been there, all that remained were a few fallen rocks.

If this was how the beast always moved around, then this was the reason why there'd been no reports of it up until now. Perhaps there had been an adventurer or two that had run into it, but they were either all dead or kept their silence, in no small part due to the sheer terror they may have felt.

If I weren't an undead, and didn't have a different mentality from most humans, I could have simply stood still, unable to move, or perhaps even wet myself in fright. Such was the sheer terror I felt.

Even though it was now a fair distance away, I could feel the earth dragon's pressure, much like sharp pinpricks on my skin. If the earth dragon's mana was like that of a lake, then my reserves of mana would be nothing more than a cup of water.

Given its massive size...even if I were to raise my sword against it, would my attacks feel like toothpicks pricking it? Would it even feel a thing? I didn't believe I could injure it, or do much of anything to it really.

An adventurer who could remain calm in the face of such an encounter... At the very least, they would have to be Platinum-class. There wasn't a single one of those individuals who were based on the fourth floor.

...Sigh.

Was my luck good today? Or was it terrible? I supposed not dying was a good thing.

I made a mental note to be more careful in the future. I really should stop putting too much confidence in my abilities, even if it were for the sake of collecting information...

Go home, Rentt. Go home.

I could no longer muster up the strength to do anything else today. All I wanted was to return home, tuck myself under clean sheets in a safe place, and sleep. Ah, and maybe I could get Lorraine to whip up some Hot Wine for me... *Yes. Let's do that, Rentt... Let's do that.*

"…An earth dragon, you say? I see you had yet another outrageous encounter, Rentt. Perhaps it's safe to assume that you're being haunted by something…" Lorraine said, exasperation and disbelief written all over her face.

After my encounter with the great beast, I left the New Moon Dungeon behind and returned back to the world above. I sold any and all perishable monster materials to the guild and went home, shaking and shivering all the way.

I kept the magic crystals and materials that weren't easily perishable, including the items required for the creation of Alize's weapons. I couldn't exactly grab a hammer and start refining the mana iron, so I'd set it aside with the intention of paying Clope a visit and putting in the appropriate customer order.

I'd take Alize along, as well. Clope had his quirks, ones I was familiar with. If the individual the weapon was being forged for wasn't present, I'd surely be bombarded with questions.

"Even I'd be willing to believe that at this point. For starters, what was an earth dragon doing there? There was no news! No news at all from the guild. Not to mention that was only the fourth floor. Isn't that strange?" I said, gulping down the Hot Wine that Lorraine had made for me. I was complaining and airing my grievances, much like any drunk adventurer at a tavern.

In truth, I wasn't really that drunk. And the earth dragon appearing had nothing to do with Lorraine. I had no intentions of complaining to her, of all people, but I just needed to voice my discontent, my outrage, at something. I just had to.

The situation I'd faced was much like that of an ogre suddenly appearing on the first floor of the Water Moon Dungeon. Or perhaps a giant horde of goblins suddenly appearing in the streets of a relatively safe city… It was an unreasonable occurrence.

No matter how much you prepared, it was simply impossible to avoid situations like that. Even if you were to escape calmly and rationally, you would first need to have the capabilities and strength of a Platinum-class adventurer, so it went without saying that I couldn't match that by any means at this point. It was impossible.

Perhaps it was because Lorraine understood how I felt, or because she'd seen through my drunken ramblings and simply let it slide, but she responded with an empathic smile.

"Well, it's not impossible for a strong monster to appear on a shallow floor... But an earth dragon on the fourth floor is truly unreasonable. It goes beyond you simply having bad luck. However... you returned with your life intact. Should you not be grateful about that? Come now. I made quite a few dishes for you to eat. How are they? Delicious?"

The table was lined with plates of food, all prepared on a much grander and more luxurious scale than usual. Each of these items was made by Lorraine's very own hands and adequately infused with some droplets of blood so they'd taste palatable to me.

The food was truly delicious, as was the wine.

No, wait. That wasn't it.

"It's delicious, but..." Was Lorraine attempting to distract me from the issue?

I looked up, looking into her eyes. She nodded curtly in response.

"Well...yes. I suppose there are some things to be concerned about. According to what you told me, Rentt, the earth dragon disappeared back into the ground...?"

"Yes. It was near what appeared to be a mining spot, like an excavation pit of some sort."

"There, you say? I see..."

Had Lorraine been down to the fourth floor before? It sounded like she recognized the place I was describing.

"Do you know of it, Lorraine...? This has been bothering me for some time... Was that place created by the dungeon to look like that?"

"...Not exactly. That facility was made by the hands of man... albeit, quite a long time ago. Just like how you ventured into the pit to excavate ore, others did the same. Mana iron was mined there, you see. That pit was most likely a purpose-built mine. Perhaps dating back a few centuries, if not thousands of years."

The discussion greatly increased in scale. If that facility had existed that long ago...did that mean Maalt didn't even exist back then? Was the dungeon that ancient?

Although I'd initially planned on developing a better understanding of the dungeon's inner workings and its monsters, delving into history was something else altogether. While I had some knowledge on the history of the Kingdom of Yaaran, and Maalt, anything regarding civilizations that came before lay firmly in the heads of specialized scholars.

"Take the mana iron we are currently talking about, for instance," Lorraine continued. "The excavation techniques of the dwarves shine when it comes to mining this particular material. If you desired a large quantity, it would be faster to get in touch with them and simply buy the required amount. However, such was the case when that excavation facility was still active. If I had to guess, mana iron was most likely a precious resource back then, and procuring it was most likely very difficult. Mana iron is still valuable today, yes, but with an increase in the amount of potential ore veins and locations you could extract it from, it's hardly as costly. If this were not the case, even if it were only the fourth floor, no civilization would purposefully build an excavation facility in a place where monsters roamed free."

Lorraine had a point. But if that were true...

"Why, then, are the items still laying there?"

"Are you asking about how they still remained where they were, or why they were still operational?"

"Both, really."

I had a hard time believing that adventurers wouldn't just make off with the items, given that they were valuable instruments. As for the items themselves, it was strange for them to continue operating now that there was no longer anyone infusing mana into them. No matter how well-made the magic item, it was all but impossible for it to continue operating indefinitely, barring some very specific exceptions.

Lorraine calmly nodded. "In truth, the answer to both those questions is one and the same. The magic items were simply consumed by the dungeon. A reasonable assumption, no? As such, anyone who attempts to bring such an item back would find it impossible to do so, and the items would continue operating for eternity. Not a system I understand very well at all, but...that's just how it is, Rentt. There is little to be done about it."

Consumed by the dungeon...

This referred to the phenomenon of dead adventurers and monsters eventually disappearing if left alone for long enough in the dungeons. Were magic items susceptible to this too?

However...considering the fact that the weapons of dead adventurers occasionally appeared in treasure chests, I supposed that wasn't too strange. But in that case...

"Are there instances of items being consumed by the dungeon, then reproduced as they were before...?"

I'd certainly heard of no such phenomenon.

"Ah, yes. There are, in fact, some examples. Not many, but enough for our purposes. Have you heard the story of Good King Felt? The king who built a city within a dungeon?"

Good King Felt... It was a story of a king who'd left his original kingdom, leading an ethnic group of citizens who were being unfairly persecuted by their kingdom. They wandered the lands, eventually chancing upon a gigantic dungeon, within which the Good King built a city... Or so the legend goes. The story was featured often in picture books, plays, and the like. Good King Felt was a well-known folk story character.

Of course I knew about him.

"Ah. I have. But what of it?"

"That is no mere story, Rentt. It is a historic record of events. I know of the dungeon that he built his city in...and there, standing to this day, is that exact same city."

"Wh-What?!" I'd never heard of anything like that.

As if anticipating my surprise, Lorraine coolly continued. "Yes, yes. I know how you must feel. However, you must keep this fact to yourself. That the story of Good King Felt is real. After all, the existence of this city is still treated as a huge secret in my own hometown to this day. If you value your life, Rentt, then surely you will remain silent?"

"Come on now..." I'd been suddenly told of this terrible secret, and now it sat in my mind.

"Given these facts," Lorraine, ignoring my protests, continued, "the case of the excavation facility is not all that strange. But of course, the only one in this kingdom who would believe in such a theory is yours truly."

"What do you mean?"

"You see, the people of this kingdom, be it the adventurer's guild, or the townsfolk of Maalt... All of them simply assume that the excavation facility on the fourth floor is an oddity created by the dungeon. But of course they would think they way. The theory of man-made magic items installed by the hands of man being absorbed by the dungeon and made to work forever... Hardly a popular theory, I would say. Do you believe in it, Rentt?"

I snorted slightly at her question. But of course I believed it. Did she even have to ask such a question?

"It's almost like you're testing me with those words, Lorraine. Surely you understand as well. There's no reason to not believe what you said. If I began doubting your words, then who would I trust? Who would so seriously investigate and research this body of mine, if not you yourself?"

I spoke true. I'd be hard-pressed to find anyone who'd believe a tale as tall as mine. In fact, I couldn't think of anyone other than Lorraine who'd actually sincerely conduct research regarding my...condition.

Hypothetically speaking, there were probably a few individuals who'd be all too eager to examine me should I show them my body and ask them to teach me its secrets. But those individuals would most likely treat me as a lab animal, a test subject, and would butcher me terribly, leaving me to wander in one research facility or other. I'd be like a caged bird for the rest of my life. At the very least, I was sure they wouldn't allow me to roam about as freely as I could now.

Lorraine smiled at my slightly heated response. "...Yes, yes. It is as you say. I apologize. Perhaps I, too, am a little drunk."

For a moment, it looked like Lorraine was staring toward an unseen place far, far away. Concerned, I inquired after her.

Lorraine shook her head slowly. "No, it is nothing. I was simply…reminiscing. About the time I spent back in my homeland. After all, the people there treated me as an oddity, an irregular, no matter what I said."

"Eh?" It was extremely rare for Lorraine to speak of her past.

Her homeland… If memory served, it was the kingdom that Lorraine had lived in before she came to Yaaran. If I could recall, it was known as the land of knowledge… Hmm, what exactly was it again?

"Your homeland… Was it the Empire of Lelmudan?"

"Yes, that's it. Quite the memory you have."

"A rural bumpkin I may be, but surely I'd remember the hometown of a dear friend. Though it is quite far, and I've never set foot on its lands."

From what I'd heard, the empire occupied a large area of land and was based somewhere in the west. In addition, the Church of Lobelia had quite the presence in the empire…

But of course, I'd heard all this from Lorraine.

The Kingdom of Yaaran, being a small kingdom in the east, hardly felt the influence of the empire. Perhaps it was more accurate to say that the Empire of Lelmudan simply had no interest in a small, boring kingdom like Yaaran. Yaaran wasn't even really known for any notable exports. The empire had nothing to gain by conquering this place…

That was what I thought, having lived for most of my life in this kingdom myself.

If the Empire of Lelmudan ever did invade Yaaran, it would be after Yaaran itself had been absorbed into some other, bigger kingdom. After all, Yaaran was a boring, rural kingdom…and that was all it was.

I felt sad just thinking of that. It wasn't *that* bad a kingdom, all things considered! Though, many other aspects of Yaaran did leave much to be desired...

Unaware of my inner monologues, Lorraine pressed on.

"Unlike the Kingdom of Yaaran, the flow of time seemed faster in that place. Now that I think of it...it was truly a tiring existence. Its citizens would work hard every day, kicking their competition to the side, or using them as stepping-stones on their way to the top. The empire was filled with such individuals. Considering that it and its citizens were reasonably prosperous, I suppose I cannot fault their approach..but it's a good example of a lack of moderation, if nothing else."

"Is that why you came here?"

Lorraine seemed to freeze up slightly at my question, but eventually she nodded.

"That was one of the bigger reasons, yes. Perhaps I could say I was simply searching for some peace... But enough of that. I lived quite the different life back in the empire than the one I do now, you see. I was quite the academic elite. If I really felt up to it, I could easily aim for the seat of chancellor at Lelmudan's First University."

I tilted my head at the unfamiliar noun. A mouthful for a country bumpkin such as myself.

"...What is this...Lelmudan First University?"

"Ah. My alma mater, I suppose. A castle of knowledge, and one of the most prestigious in the empire. However, anyone could enroll so long as they worked hard. Not too impressive from that angle, no... The seat of Chancellor was the one that was most desired among the empire's academics—well, one of them, anyway. I, too, was no exception. I attempted to obtain that very same seat for myself. Many things happened, and I had quite a few achievements under my belt.

However…there were quite a few individuals who got in my way, for the purposes of obstructing my research of course. I'd laid out some truths in ways anyone could understand. However, those individuals denied whatever I said with all their might.

"Do you understand, Rentt? Suppose that there is an orange before you. I claim that it's an orange, right? But then someone comes along and says it is an apple. Before long, another will claim that it's a loaf of bread…and the naysayers simply continue to multiply. Soon enough, I would be seen as the one in the wrong, as far as public perception would go anyway. Even so, no matter how I looked at it, the object before me was none other than an orange. One could lose their mind thinking about all this."

"That's…"

It was all too familiar a tale. At least, I knew that much of human subtleties to understand it.

In other words, there were people who were discontent with the pace at which Lorraine was rising to the top, and quite a number of them at that. Although you couldn't discount the possibility that the person in question sincerely didn't believe that they were looking at an orange, in this case it was obvious they were trying to prevent Lorraine from reaching her goal.

What a terrible series of events, I thought…and perhaps this showed on my face, for Lorraine chuckled softly in response.

"Well…I suppose I was bad at dealing with people back then. I was just a child. Perhaps I'd be able to react better as I am now… I think so anyway. Now that I think back on it, it wasn't too terrible a place, you know. Though it was still a trying place to be… I was tired about so many things, which is why I came here. Suddenly, and out of the blue… Somehow, it just happened that way."

"…Was that not reckless of you, Lorraine? From what I heard, it seemed like you were in charge of some important work."

"And so it was, yes. However…if I had not done so, I would have surely lost some degree of my sanity. I wanted to say goodbye to those days, to that boredom and the constant feeling of irritation that plagued me. Honestly speaking, I felt a sense of release after coming here. It was a sort of mental stimulation I hadn't felt in such a long time, and I was excited. It was good that I came to Maalt, yes… And, of course, this was where I met you."

While I'd known all this time that Lorraine was a scholar from Lelmudan, who'd come all the way to Maalt because she'd gotten sick of her previous life, this was the first time I heard about it in such detail.

I never really believed Lorraine's tale about how she was just some second-rate scholar from Lelmudan, reassigned to Yaaran without any title to show for it. I'd known her for over a decade now and bore witness to her academic and technical prowess firsthand.

I'd discussed the possibility of Lorraine becoming a court scholar in Yaaran before, just with a little bit more effort of course. Lorraine, however, was never too keen or pleased with that prospect, and I eventually stopped bringing it up altogether. I had supposed Lorraine had no interest in factional infighting and politics…but I never imagined that she came from such circumstances.

Even so…I now greatly preferred that Lorraine remained here instead. After all, she'd helped me countless times and was my closest friend in the township of Maalt.

No matter your past, all you had to do was enjoy your days from here on out.

For some reason, this was what I thought as I finished the rest of my meal.

The next day...

Plans were in place for me to meet the auctioneer staff at the Stheno Company. The subject of our discussion was none other than the issue of the tarasque materials. To think that the items would sell for several times their estimated auction value... I found myself looking forward to this.

The problem was the issue of the buyer. What kind of person were they...? The rich and powerful often had certain discriminatory views. In fact, many of them were quite strange, and this realization caused some degree of fear to creep into my being.

Perhaps they would be an idiosyncratic, whimsical person, much like Laura was. But that didn't seem very possible... Laura was, after all, a bit of an exception.

Then there was the issue of evaluating the materials I'd collected yesterday. I had to show them all to Lorraine for a once-over since it was impossible for me to gauge if those materials were acceptable just by looking at them. They were most likely quite all right, is what I thought.

The reason I put this off for a day was because I'd returned very late the night before. Then there was the sheer amount of materials I'd brought back to consider, as well...

"Ah. Already awake, Rentt?" Lorraine asked as she entered the living room, leaving her bedroom behind.

She wasn't in her pajamas, though. She'd already changed, looking how she always did, in her mage-like attire.

I could never really grasp if Lorraine was a morning person or not. But thinking about it, the only times she was sleepy was when she burned the midnight oil, working on some experiment or research document. I guessed she was a morning person in that case.

"Yes. The amount of time I spend sleeping has shortened drastically ever since I became an undead. In fact, as a ghoul, I hardly slept at all."

"You do sleep a bit now, right? To think that you now require sleep after going through Existential Evolution... Quite interesting. Perhaps you are closer than ever to becoming human again, Rentt."

"I'd be glad if that were the case..."

There was no way of knowing for certain, though. I was capable of sleeping as and when I desired and could wake up whenever I felt like I should. I hadn't actually tried it, but I felt like that was very well within my capabilities.

"Becoming more human is one thing, but to have your sleep shortened...I'm envious, Rentt. Too many a time have I been ambushed by sleep just when I got to the best part of an experiment... Alas. I suppose it's simply a necessity of mankind."

"Ever the scholar, I see. But I like sleeping. I'd love to return to a body in which I could sleep well again. I can only sleep lightly now, and I only do it because this body requires it. It's hardly enjoyable..."

Even so, the fact remained that I was capable of sleep, and I ended up sleeping one way or another. It was difficult to break free from an ingrained habit.

While becoming an undead brought with it many advantages, I noticed that I'd also lost quite a few things. The capability to enjoy a good night's rest was one of them.

"An interesting topic, in many ways. But we should set that aside for now. You were going to show me the materials, yes? And of course, the mana iron has to be refined as well," Lorraine said, interrupting the conversation.

It was a conversation we could have anytime, so I supposed she was right to hold off on it for now. We were somewhat short on time.

It wasn't simply about showing her the materials on hand. Lorraine had to go through the trouble of extracting the mana iron, forming the metal into blocks via alchemy. What I had extracted were rocks containing veins of mana iron within, not refined ingots. The ore that I had harvested was high in purity, but it wasn't something that could be used immediately without any processing.

I could take the ore to the Blacksmith's Guild, but that would cost me a fair amount of coin. While I'd excavated the ore myself with the aim of saving money, unexpected expenses crept up at every corner. Honestly speaking, while part of this excavation trip was out of consideration for my disciple, Alize, spending some coin on creating the weapon was fine. However, since Lorraine was capable of refining the ore as well, I decided to simply leave it to her expertise. I could just pay her any fees that may occur. Knowing her, though, she'd most likely refuse payment for something so simple.

"Yes, but it's by no means a huge amount…" Saying so, I placed each of the materials onto the table.

This was Lorraine's experimental table, which was wider and larger than her dining table. There was more than enough space for me to lay out the spoils. But I wasn't going to just dump everything on the table. For now, the magic crystals and mana iron ore would do. I'd have to pull out the lumber collected from the ents piece by piece, and they were large pieces as well. Although shrub ents were commonly the size of shrubs, stacking piece after piece of lumber on the table would quickly get unwieldy.

"Quite a few things here and there, eh, Rentt? Hmm… This is an orc soldier's magic crystal, I suppose?"

CHAPTER 2: MATERIALS FOR MY DISCIPLE'S WEAPON

As expected of Lorraine, she was able to tell which monster it came from by size alone.

While magic crystals had quite a few distinctive characteristics, including color and shape, to be able to identify the monster it came from just by looking at a crystal was surprisingly difficult to do. At the very least, I couldn't do it.

However, the quality of a crystal was easy to discern at a glance. This was an important fact, considering quality was often linked to price. The ability to tell if a crystal was worth much was what truly defined you as an adventurer. Those who were able to precisely identify a crystal, however, were in another class altogether. The dissection chambers staff, or hobbyists who loved to collect crystals... And Lorraine, of course. These people had an almost encyclopedic knowledge of magic crystals.

"Yes. This one came from the second floor."

"The second floor? Ho... Then perhaps a flood is imminent, yes? Rare monsters appear in such events...and I do look forward to it, but..."

"You shouldn't be enjoying floods at all, Lorraine. It'd be best if it didn't happen in the first place."

That said, floods weren't too dangerous so long as the adequate preparations were made. If the flood were severe, it was very possible for it to wipe out nearby towns and cities, but such occurrences were rare.

"True, yes, but no matter how much one struggles, floods are bound to happen. In which case, would it not be more advantageous to enjoy them?"

"Well... I suppose. If you put it that way."

"Ah, yes, as for the mana iron... Hmm. As expected, Rentt. This is some good-quality ore... Hmm? This is...?"

Lorraine raised up a piece of ore she held in her hand. She stared at it for a while, saying nothing.

"What is it, Lorraine?" I asked as she continued inspecting the piece.

"Do you not see the difference in color?"

As she said, there were traces of yellow in the mana iron ore piece. Mana iron, from what I knew, was usually more purplish in color. Why, then, were there traces of yellow in this rock? How mysterious...

"Could you explain?"

"If I had to guess... You excavated this where the earth dragon was, yes? Most likely, the mana of that creature changed the characteristics of the metal within. After all, mana iron is highly sensitive to mana, even without any refinement. Even so...such a pronounced example is somewhat rare..."

"Do you mean to say it's no longer usable as mana iron...?"

If that really were the case, I'd have wasted my entire excavation trip. To think I'd given it my all, shaking all the way as I ran home after escaping the earth dragon... Now they were all unusable? This was too much.

Lorraine, however, quickly assuaged my fears.

"Not to worry, Rentt. To begin with, there are quite a few pieces in here that haven't been affected. If you ever need mana iron in the future, we can simply draw from this supply. However, the affected pieces..."

"Are they defective after all?"

"Nothing like that. In fact, it is quite the opposite. Mana iron that has been altered by an earth dragon's mana... This type of material would easily fetch a large sum of coin. You could smelt weapons or equipment from it. Magic items, even. Perhaps they might even come with a special effect or two."

"A...special effect, you say?"

Lorraine nodded. "I cannot be absolutely sure that this piece in my hands will have the same effect, but... A sword forged of enchanted ore like this could very well summon spears of rock and earth without expending the user's mana. In other words, this ore could be used to smelt enchanted swords, armor...even magic items of the same vein. The possibility is somewhat high."

Enchanted swords and armor... Basically, equipment that had been enchanted with strong magic. They would be special pieces, indeed. They were exceedingly rare, and if you were to purchase them, you best prepare for several platinum pieces to disappear from your wallet.

However, all that said, there were actually quite a few individuals who used such weapons. They were either very skilled, or very wealthy. A second-rate adventurer much like myself would usually have nothing to do with items like that. If I were to ever wield such an item, it'd be after slaving away at numerous requests, saving up a large sum of coin. Or perhaps I'd increase my adventurer rank, become famous, and receive it as a reward from a client. Oh, or perhaps I'd be lucky, and find one in a chest in a dungeon.

To actually craft such a weapon, however...

I supposed there was some value in having run into the earth dragon after all, despite the ever-looming terror of death.

There was a problem, however. Crafting with such material was no doubt incredibly expensive... There was no way I could come up with such funds. Would I have enough after selling the tarasque materials?

I could discuss all this with Clope at the smithy, but even so, I couldn't ask for too much of a discount. Hard work and skill should be compensated in kind.

Until I had enough coin to smelt it, this ore would just be sitting here in the meantime. I made a mental note to at least discuss this with Clope later.

"...I suppose this goes without saying, but this enchanted ore can't be used as a base for Alize's weapon, right?"

"Perhaps somewhere down the road, Rentt. I, however, would not recommend you gift something like this to her right away. It wouldn't do her any good, from an educational standpoint. If she were to wield a strong weapon from the get-go, a weapon much more capable than her...she may very well form misconceived notions about her own capabilities."

I supposed that was true. However, even if I were to hypothetically create enchanted equipment from this ore, I didn't feel capable of using such powerful equipment at this point. Perhaps I'd be worthy of such a weapon if I got just a little bit stronger... But of course, I still wasn't quite there. In that case, the idea of an enchanted weapon would have to be shelved for a while.

But...if I saved up enough money, I'd very much like to craft such a weapon. I really wanted to swing it around as well.

...To prevent Alize from becoming an adventurer with such bad perspectives, it would be prudent that her first weapon not be forged from such a material, I thought.

"Well, then... I'll discuss this with Clope later. Now, for the remaining ingredients. I collected quite a few types of lumber from the shrub ents... Would these do as materials for the wands?"

I arranged the magic crystals and ore neatly on one side of the table and placed down the pieces of wood I'd gathered from the ents. I didn't take out everything, of course, just a sample from each. These were fragments that splintered off during the battle. I arranged the fragments on the table, deciding to take out the actual pieces later.

Lorraine glanced at the samples on the table before turning to me. "Birch, fir, and…ebony. I see. I thought you might bring back some strange lumber or another, but I see you have unexpectedly returned with useful materials."

I'd been praised for my efforts.

Actually…was that praise at all? It was almost as if Lorraine had expected the worst, for some reason or other…

"What do you mean by 'strange lumber'…?"

"Lumber that was not strong enough or difficult to work with. I assumed that would happen. My fault, yes, for not warning you beforehand about them. What you brought this time isn't bad at all. However, ebony may be a little too heavy for someone of Alize's stature. Birch or fir will suffice for our purposes."

Come to think of it, the ebony shrub ent had been somewhat heavier than the other two. While I hadn't had to exert much strength to place the materials into my magic bag, each of its blows in combat had carried with it a certain sense of weight.

…*Hmm?*

"Was ebony a bad choice for a wand then…?"

"To some extent, yes. However, it would actually be a good fit for you. After all, you have the strength for it. And you most likely swing your weapons with considerable force. Ebony is a relatively strong material, so that alone would not break it. A good fit for you indeed. But it's a difficult material to work with… It will be a challenge, Rentt!" Lorraine said, with a somewhat mischievous smile on her face.

…Well. I had collected this lumber myself, after all. I supposed I could have her shoulder the responsibility in this particular case.

"And the magic crystal…?"

"Spoiled for choice, yes? Do not hesitate too much, Rentt. Simply pick the color you like. I will have Alize do the same when she crafts hers."

The crystals I could use were either that of the mina goblins, orc soldier, or terra drake. Other than those, all the others were harvested from the first or second floors. Lorraine had specified that only one from the third floor or below would work.

"I wanted to ask… Is the magic crystal of a goblin or slime simply unusable in wands?"

"I wouldn't say so. It is not impossible by any means… But there would certainly be issues with the amplification and control of mana, among other things. Alize, in particular, has large reserves of mana within her. If we used such simple crystals, even basic spells from Alize would almost certainly cause it to crack."

"…Unable to contain her mana, I suppose."

"You could say that, yes. However, if one has been utilizing mana for a long time, it's possible for one to moderate their own mana flow. In that case, even a wand made with such a weak crystal could last quite a while. But it goes without saying that Alize hardly has the required experience. Hence, it is impossible."

Now I understood. Since it was to be regularly used in practice, it'd be a big problem if it continuously broke. Considerable effort was required, and another wand would have to be made, should such a thing happen.

While I'd heard stories of mages breaking multiple wands while learning how to craft them, magic crystals on cracked wands often exploded when used. Quite the hazard. There was no need to go out of your way to court such danger.

"With that being the case, Rentt, may I take all these magic crystals?"

I nodded. I'd gathered all these for the lesson, after all. While the responsibility for gathering the required materials for the lesson originally laid with the teacher—in this case, Lorraine—she'd offered to pay me for my field work.

I, however, refused to accept any payment. To begin with, I was paying both Alize's and my own lesson fees. If anything, I was deeper in debt to Lorraine.

Lorraine was, of course, a most capable mage. Under normal circumstances, it was impossible to receive such tuition without paying a large sum up front.

However, I couldn't simply accept a monetary reward for my efforts. Lorraine protested my decision, saying I should take what was given. Even so, I insisted on not taking any payment.

Lorraine was insistent on giving some coin for my efforts, but I was insistent in my refusal as well. In that case, we should probably just give each other some leeway and not charge for services either way. And I had no intentions of simply mooching off Lorraine's goodwill.

In reality, however, I felt like I had already done plenty of that...

After our short discussion about payment, Lorraine continued. "Well, then, next is the refinement of the mana iron ore."

Ore refinement...

There were quite a few ways to go about doing it. For instance, the blacksmith's guild often housed magic items for this purpose— the large-scale refinement of ore. This was probably the most well-known method. There were older, more primitive methods that didn't rely on magic or magic items, but they were more expensive, and also took much more time.

In border settlements, small-scale refinement operations were often present. Larger ones were somewhat rare. Yaaran was a rural border kingdom, so I could very well find a small-scale ore refining operation in a mountain village somewhere, though I wasn't sure if I'd ever have the opportunity.

As such, most ore was refined with the aid of magic items. However, there was yet another way to go about it:

Alchemy.

Strictly speaking, refining ore with magic items was considered alchemical in nature as well. After all, those items were made with alchemy. It was, however, possible to control your mana to perform the refinement without specialized items. This was the very same method that Lorraine was going to utilize.

Alchemy was by no means restricted to mages alone. There were alchemists who weren't mages. But having some degree of control over your mana made research in the alchemical arts all the easier. If one lacked this control, they'd have to use certain magic crystals, or specialized magic items that moderated mana. It was all quite troublesome.

Lorraine, being the skilled mage she was, was capable of performing the refinement process with only one hand, and perhaps one eye closed. In fact, that's exactly what Lorraine was currently doing. Her hands were placed on some pieces of mana iron ore on the table.

"Well, then. Without further ado..." Saying so, Lorraine concentrated. The process had begun.

I couldn't understand it, given that I couldn't even see where Lorraine's mana was currently being focused. But the ore soon reacted to her mana and gave off a faint, purplish glow. Soon after, its form began changing. The glowing parts of the ore seemingly dissolved and became a glowing liquid. That was most likely the purified mana iron.

Like a series of snakes, the veins of mana iron began peeling away from the rock.

Soft clattering could be heard as small fragments of impurities flew out of the liquefied mana iron. The purified mana iron snaked and flowed, slowly gathering into a puddle on the table. The puddle grew, and it became a large, metallic piece.

"…Hmm. I suppose this is all," Lorraine said, grasping a rectangular piece of purple metal as it floated in the air.

"You're done?" I asked.

"Yes, Rentt, it is finished. Quite well done, if I do say so myself. I am not one to toot my own horn, but most alchemists are not capable of creating an ingot of such high purity, I'd wager."

With that, Lorraine extended her arm, handing the mana iron ingot over to me. I stared at it. Despite Lorraine's joke about being overconfident in her work, the ingot was, in fact, very well made. I couldn't say with certainty exactly how refined an ingot was once it reached a certain point, but a single glance was enough for me to know that the piece I was holding had a much higher point of purity compared to one obtained from, say, the blacksmith's guild.

But of course, the latter was a mass-produced product, whereas the ingot I held in my hands wasn't. The methodology employed was different as well. Considering the fact that a smelter usually improved upon the quality of ingots after receiving them from the guild, it was simply impossible to compare the two.

The piece I held in my hands was of a much higher quality. All in all, Lorraine had done more than well enough on her task.

"I may as well deal with all the other pieces now too. Would you prefer that, Rentt?" Lorraine asked.

I nodded in response, emptying out all the mana iron ore pieces in my bag onto the table. "Ah… Some of the enchanted pieces are in here as well. I'll split them up. Other than the yellowed pieces, should I just gather all the rest?"

"Ah, yes, the enchanted ore. While there will be some pieces with alterations on the inside, I can deal with that during the process. I could do all of it at once, but it is indeed tiring. Splitting them up would be the wiser choice here."

Lorraine was more than capable of purifying both the normal mana iron and the ore that had been enchanted with the earth dragon's mana. The latter was apparently more mana-intensive, however, so I set about separating them.

From what Lorraine said, the chance of failure was much higher should the two be mixed together. A trace amount wouldn't take too much effort to remove, though. With that in mind, I neatly organized the ore pieces at hand.

"So many…"

Lorraine wasn't referring to the amount of mana iron on the table, but to the enchanted ore that had been tinted with the earth dragon's mana. About a third of the pieces were that way. From what I could see, quite a few ingots could be created.

"Are you sure this earth dragon of yours did not simply release a wave of mana into its surroundings? Normal adventurers would most likely have passed out had they been present…" Lorraine said, ever so casually stating a terrifying fact.

It may very well have been due to this body of mine that I didn't suffer any ill effects. A normal adventurer wouldn't have died had they been present, but they could have been attacked by monsters in the vicinity after passing out, which would eventually lead to their deaths.

"No point dallying, yes?"

Lorraine placed her hands over the pile of normal mana iron and began focusing once more. Her progress was much faster this time around. Perhaps she'd developed a better understanding of the metal's structure.

Ingot after ingot piled up on the table.

"…All right, then. This is all we get," Lorraine said, about half an hour after the purification process had started.

She was incredibly fast. The average alchemist, in comparison, would take a full day to do what Lorraine had just done before my eyes.

"Next would be…this."

Lorraine placed her hands over the enchanted ore. I could sense her concentrating as the ore began responding.

"Will you be all right, Lorraine…?"

I couldn't help but be worried. The sheer speed at which she worked was somewhat intimidating.

"Ha. This is nothing…" Lorraine said as ingots began piling up once more.

Unlike the purple mana iron ingots that I was now used to seeing, these new ingots were yellow. Yellow, but also purer in appearance. While their glow was somewhat faint, I could feel a certain sense of pressure—an aura that was absent from the normal mana iron ingots. Was it just my imagination?

"All right, then. I suppose we are done," Lorraine said after ten minutes, a significant decrease from the batch before. Even so, her work was perfect, as far as I could tell.

"As expected of you, Lorraine. But for you to do all this for free… I feel guilty."

I would've expected to spend at least one gold coin if I'd gone to an average alchemist. It'd take them a day to do this, and the purity of the ore meant that a large amount of mana was required for the job.

Lorraine just shook her head. "Should I be feeling guilty for the fact that I am researching a unique existence in the world then? One that could not be found anywhere else? Surely such an experience would be worth a thousand pieces of gold coins, if not more. After all, it's very possible to find an alchemist who is capable of doing what I just did, but it's impossible to find a being such as yourself. Don't worry too much about it, Rentt."

Was I the only one of my kind? At the very least, I hadn't met anyone else who was quite like me, and neither had Lorraine. The prerequisite of being eaten whole by a dragon was quite the tall barrier to entry in and of itself...

"Well, then, I suppose we could consider this a fair exchange of services?"

Lorraine nodded at my suggestion, and that was that.

Chapter 3:   The Stheno Company

"Well, then. Go forth cautiously, Rentt. You know how merchants are, yes? They cover all their bases," Lorraine said, glancing at me.

"Yes. I think I understand that very well..."

I'd done this several times in life—obtaining a valuable item of some kind and speaking to a merchant from a large company about it, that is. At least, I assumed that was Lorraine's intent. But she shook her head.

"It's different from how things were before, Rentt. As you are now, your body is in and of itself a valuable item. Have your wits about you...as if you were walking around with, say, a hundred platinum pieces."

Hmm... Lorraine had a point. While most would either attempt to capture or slay a vampire should one appear before them, merchants would certainly go for the former. The adventurers they hired as bodyguards were often extremely capable as well. It'd be most troublesome if they were summoned.

I steeled myself. I had to be very careful.

...Not that I was going to be careless in the first place. I just had to be that extra bit more cautious.

"I understand. Well, then, I'll be going now."

With a casual wave, I left Lorraine's abode behind, walking out onto the streets of Maalt.

Located on a busy road, and in a relatively conspicuous location, was the main building of the Stheno Company. The building was quite large, just what I'd expect from one of Maalt's top merchant companies.

It was a brick and stone affair, five floors tall. The first two floors housed shops and the like, while the upper levels housed the company's administrative centers and warehouses. Judging by the consistent flow of individuals in and out of its doors, it was plain to see the company had no shortage of customers. It sold everything from daily grocery goods to tools for adventurers, and a little bit of everything else. The selection was colorful, to say the least.

I was among the customers near the entrance of the store. Few were masked and robed like me, though. Some had robes or masks on, yes, but I failed to spot another customer with a mask that stood out as much as my skull-shaped one.

Most of these masked customers were victims of burns or scars, so their masks were used as a means of obscuring their injuries. From these customers in particular I felt gazes of pity. I'd heard in the past that individuals with particularly large and ornate masks were respected in this strange way.

Even so, while there were some individuals with fancy masks, they usually had an equally fanciful outfit to boot. Someone such as myself, with an ornate mask and a relatively simple robe instead stood out more, like a sore thumb.

But I couldn't just stand here and do nothing. I was now at the entrance to the Stheno Company's main building. Should I enter as is? Due to the fact that I usually operated late at night or early in the morning—or at least in the less crowded hours of the afternoon—

standing in the thick of such crowds was new to me. It was somewhat nostalgic, but I found myself nervous, wondering if I should change my attire. Perhaps this place unsettled me more deeply than my encounter with the earth dragon…

Bah. That was an exaggeration. *You stood up to such a beast! Why would you be terrified of a normal crowd of people?*

With that, I walked straight into the entrance and through the doors.

"Welcome, welcome, dear customer! What may I assist you with today?"

As soon as I stepped through the doors, a voice called out to me. Soon enough, a lanky man approached me. There was a sense of professionalism about him. While he wasn't running, I could tell from the cadence of his steps that he was an adventurer.

As expected of a large, flagship store… Even its employees were something else.

Average stores were different; you could enter and leave as you pleased. Honestly, I preferred such stores, but if you desired items of a certain refinement and quality, a store such as this was much more reliable.

There was a reassuring presence about the man. It felt like you could leave their entire shopping list to him, and he'd select only the most fitting items for the purpose. Such an establishment could, of course, sell someone everything they didn't need. But then again, an establishment of this level most likely understood that doing such a thing would simply serve to thin their consumer base.

"Ah… Hmm. Ahem. Yes. I am known as Rentt Vivie. I was the one who had slain a tarasque prior…"

Upon hearing my name, the man appeared convinced but quickly cut me off mid-sentence.

"I have been informed of your arrival, sir. Please, this way," the staff member said, leading me to the back of store.

This area was no longer part of the sales floor but instead a landing for an elevator of sorts, presumably one that we'd take to the administrative offices of the building.

"I haven't been to this establishment for a while. To think that something like this now exists here…" I said, looking at the elevator in surprise.

"Ah, yes. We've recently received and installed this contraption, you see. It was built by artisans—craftsmen of magic items from the capital. Only this particular store in Maalt has such an installation. But…you *have* been to the store before, sir? Do excuse me, but how long has it been since your last visit…?"

Craftsmen of magic items from the capital, huh…

I'd read about elevators in one of Lorraine's tomes before, but this was the first time I was seeing one in the flesh. From what I could recall, these machines were created by techniques from the western lands. At one point, I'd wondered when Yaaran would adopt such technologies, but it seemed like it had already done so.

If there was an elevator in a border town like Maalt, would that mean there were many such machines in the capital, then? Hmm… Given that they could only be created by certain craftsmen, I supposed they weren't all that common. A show of power from this particular establishment perhaps? A declaration of wealth?

More importantly, this staff member was now asking about my last visit. Was he able to recall the faces of all his customers?

Well, I could have very well spoken with another staff member instead of this particular man and still be asked the same. I just didn't remember too well. Perhaps it was a requirement of this particular establishment, for staff to remember their customers.

Even so, this was a particularly troublesome question for me. I had to quickly come up with some excuse.

"When was it indeed... Perhaps it was another store instead of this one. If I recall, I visited with the intent of purchasing Maaltan Magnolia leaves..."

"Ah, in that case, kind sir, you're most likely referring to the Witta Company. That particular establishment stocks many items geared toward adventurers. Items of a respectable quality too. Of course, our store will serve your needs equally well, if not better."

As the man said, Maaltan Magnolia leaves were only sold by the Witta Company. Stheno didn't carry them. But of course, that was only an excuse on my part. The staff member, however, seemed convinced, a relief for me.

On another note, those leaves weren't exactly an item that flew off the shelves. It was largely up to the store if they offered it for sale to begin with. It was a bit of a necessity to us adventurers, however, and the Witta Company had been stocking them since times of old. Due to the strong association between item and store, other shops didn't often carry them, if at all.

Since these plants grew abundantly around Maalt, it was easy enough for Stheno's staff to sell them, but given that most adventurers simply bought them from Witta, there wasn't much point. There were many other products that brought customers to their door.

Honestly, they had enough customers as is. It was hardly a problem for the Stheno Company.

"...We have arrived, sir. This is the fifth floor of our store. The meeting room is this way, if you would," the man said, guiding me once again as we stepped out of the elevator.

Finally, we stopped outside a set of double wooden doors—relatively expensive-looking doors at that.

Well, not so much expensive-looking. The doors themselves were probably worth quite the sum in coin. They were adorned with intricate, ornate carvings, and the knobs seemed to be made of solid silver. Was it this fanciful because it was a meeting room, or was the company simply that well-off...?

Whatever the case...

"Please, this way."

With a click, the knob turned, and the doors opened. I stepped through as instructed, and the man soon closed the doors behind us.

"Do make yourself comfortable, sir," the staff member said, ushering me toward a plush-looking sofa. He soon fetched an elaborate tea set from a shelf in the room, the set exuding an air of elegance and a warm, gentle fragrance.

"Black tea, sir. Brewed with the best leaves our establishment has to offer. If you'd like, here are some other offerings that pair well with the tea. Now, if you'll excuse me, kind sir, I shall fetch my master. Please, make yourself comfortable during this time."

Saying so, the man bowed deeply, quietly leaving the room.

"Hmm... Delicious. These little snacks here, too..."

Momentarily lost in the delectable world of snacks and tea tidbits, I was unceremoniously surprised by a few loud knocks on the door. Panicking, I quickly placed the teacup back on its saucer, did what I could to calm myself, and responded in a cautious voice.

"...Please enter."

"Do excuse me then…"

With that, a large, round-bellied man entered the room. His clothing was vibrant, colors fitting of a merchant. His entire being and presence announced that he was an individual of particular import. If I had to guess, this was none other than the head of the Stheno Company.

Or, was my guess incorrect…? Fortunately, my assumptions were soon proven.

"So, you are the adventurer who slayed that tarasque… Sir Rentt Vivie, correct? I do apologize for requesting your presence in such a sudden and brusque manner. I am the head of the Stheno Company, Sharl Stheno. With regards to these developments…I do express my sincerest apologies. If you'd like, sir, we intend to offer you discounts at our establishment, along with other means of compensation and benefits that may be of use to you…"

With that, Sharl Stheno bowed his head.

Even I felt somewhat bad at suddenly having been offered so many beneficial conditions right from the get-go. I was suspicious, however. Was there something else about this arrangement that I didn't know of...?

Under normal circumstances, concessions like these were usually given during negotiations on price and the like; at least, that was how it was when I'd sold rare items to various merchant companies in the past. And yet...

Were the tarasque materials simply that respectable? Or did the individual who desired the materials simply wield that much power? Whatever the case, I couldn't let my guard down here. It was a rather exasperating thought.

I reshaped my mask so the bottom half of my face showed. Without allowing my true emotions to surface, I instead laughed, addressing the merchant casually.

"Bronze-class adventurer, Rentt Vivie, at your service. Also, about the current state of affairs... There's no need for all that really. After all, I was the one who decided to show up here today. To think the tarasque I'd worked so hard to slay would now be sold for several times the estimated auction value... Honestly, no adventurer would be displeased at this. In fact, I was so happy that I skipped all the way here to your establishment today."

The merchant laughed upon hearing the tail end of my statement.

"An unexpectedly casual person you are, Sir Rentt. Quite different from what the rumors say. They painted you as a more, how you say...rigid person."

That was a statement I couldn't ignore. Just how far had the rumors about me spread? I decided to pursue this line of inquiry.

"Rumors, you say? What kind? To be frank, I don't really have a good sense of these things, you see. What other people think of me and such…"

Perhaps I'd been well known as Rentt Faina, but as I was now…

The amount of people I interacted with had significantly decreased. Other than Lorraine, Clope, and some others, I had almost no interactions with normal adventurers. Maybe I'd picked up an object or two that adventurers dropped and returned it to them. The conversation wouldn't be particularly deep in that case.

It wasn't that I didn't want to speak to them, but there was the ever-present danger of my secret being discovered had I lingered. Sharl, on the other hand…

"Hmmm… Sir Rentt. As a merchant, revealing one's sources is really not respectable behavior, but this specific incident has been entirely brought about by us. I mentioned concessions before, correct? I shall deliver upon them. Well…to start…"

Oh. What an unexpectedly empathetic merchant…

"Where to begin?" Sharl continued. "Honestly speaking, Sir Rentt, it was surprisingly difficult to gather information about you. We knew you were an adventurer—that much was simple. But we didn't know what sort of individual you were. However, and I don't agree with this, good sir, the voices of the masses describe you as 'a most fearsome individual'…"

"Whatever do you mean by that?"

"Although you are a Bronze-class adventurer, you hardly speak to anyone. Perhaps, then, you could just be a reserved individual who doesn't care much for others? However, other adventurers who have witnessed your movements and behavior in the dungeons didn't see the skill of a Bronze-class adventurer, but something more."

I see… The occasional adventurer I'd crossed paths with… I supposed some had passed me, too, when I was locked in combat.

It was one of the dungeon's rules to not involve yourself with someone you didn't know. But even then, there was nothing to stop an adventurer from sneakily observing another. Depending on the situation, an adventurer may even *openly* observe another's battles. It wasn't a polite thing to do, but it was by no means prohibited. Most adventurers didn't pay it much heed as long as the spectator didn't get in their way.

Sharl must have obtained his information in such a fashion by speaking to the adventurers I'd crossed paths with somewhere along the way.

But…reserved and didn't care much about others? I didn't speak very much…other than to Sheila at the guild at least. Then there was Dario at the dissection chambers, though he was the one in charge there, and I didn't really speak with anyone else…

Hmm… Did I seem like an individual without any friends?

In truth, I really didn't have any. If I had to point at someone and declare that they were my friend… Well, there was Lorraine.

I shouldn't be thinking too deeply about it. I could already feel myself getting lonely.

It was true, however, that I had many friends in life.

"It seems you're giving much praise! Though I'm no one that noteworthy. After all, there are many others who are on my same level…"

I wasn't being humble here. Honestly speaking, if I had to estimate my own capabilities, perhaps I'd be a lower Silver-class adventurer, or at least somewhere around there? While I did have quite a few aces up my sleeve, and occasionally displayed explosive bursts of potential, that wasn't quite the case under normal circumstances in my day-to-day.

If anything, though, the gulf between Rentt Faina and myself was suitably large. I also had the firm belief that I would become stronger from here on out. It was a good thing.

Sharl nodded at my words. "I heard such rumors as well. I also heard that you are very efficient, Sir Rentt. You're not only strong, but you don't leave any openings for your foes. You don't fight losing battles, or so they say... And that the aura of fixation... Determination, I suppose? It seems almost...inhuman. Not that I understand the last point very well myself, Sir Rentt..."

Not fighting losing battles... I did escape if it looked like things were about to take a turn for the worse. Strangely, that seemed to be held in high regard.

As for the determination... Did I really come across that way? Hmm. I did want to try my hardest and give it my all, but I had no intentions of releasing this strange...aura? At all.

As for the comment on me seeming inhuman... Well. I wasn't human to begin with—not that I could say that, of course. Though I momentarily wondered if I could test Sharl with such a statement, just to see his reaction. If I did that, however, my life in human society would instantly end. Even if it were something brought up in jest, to be taken lightly... I couldn't be that flippant.

"Hmm... So basically, the masses see me as a coward and a dangerous individual? Something along those lines? It seems like I have no noteworthy traits then."

"Why would you interpret it in such a way, Sir Rentt...? Whatever the case...perhaps we could leave that aside. Though, there was something that I simply couldn't find out, no matter how much we dug," Sharl said, shaking his head slowly, one hand on his forehead.

I tilted my head to one side in confusion. "Hmm? And what might that be?"

"Your birthplace, Sit Rentt. Well, we know that you are from the Lelmudan Empire, but we couldn't find out much more than that. Could I perhaps ask where you were born?"

"Huh...? I, Rentt Faina, a person from the Lelmudan Empire?" was what I wanted to say. However, I'd heard that Lorraine and Sheila cooperated to cover up my background somewhat, so I wasn't all that surprised.

Sheila, who had access to records at the adventurer's guild, had most likely altered certain documents and registered this information with Lorraine's assistance. If I had to guess, my close ties with Lorraine most likely made it seem that I was from the same place she was. Adventurers often came from dubious backgrounds, but such was the nature of the job.

I could have just told Sharl the truth, but that was something I couldn't casually do with a merchant. I was a little strange, yes, but few individuals would investigate someone so intensely. It was good that we'd done all the little things we had when establishing my identity. In fact, me meeting with a merchant like this was also one of the many scenarios Lorraine had dreamed up.

"It's nothing all that mysterious, ha. Have you heard of the Mechanical City of Aavan? In the Lelmudan Empire, of course."

I knew nothing about it. I'd never even been there. Lorraine had spoken to me of the place, which was how I had come to know about it.

For instance, I knew it was a city of iron, magic, and oil. It was well developed, with magic items and machines of all types. Within it was a plethora of mechanics and mages. They were workers and craftsmen who produced new products, working around the clock, all day every day. It was a place that had attracted many individuals looking for work. Though I didn't know if this was the reason for the amount of orphans in Aavan, working as servants and assistants.

Many individuals would travel to Aavan from the slums, attracted by the prospect of obtaining some means to feed themselves. I, too, would be one of these orphans—or so my story went.

With that, I described the atmosphere and smells of Aavan, details I remembered from sketches Lorraine had shown me of the place. Sharl, for his part, seemed convinced.

"I see. So it was something like that…"

It was impossible to tell with a simple glance if the merchant believed my words. But it seemed like my words were somewhat convincing. I'd answered quite a few of his questions, and didn't make any fatal mistakes…hopefully.

I made a mental note to ask Lorraine about the quality of my responses later.

"It seems we've had quite a lengthy discussion, Sir Rentt," Sharl continued. "I feel like I now have a better grasp of your personality. Alas, the time is upon us. The individual coming to speak with you will be arriving soon… Is that all right with you?"

Just as I nodded at his question…

Knock, knock…

A few swift raps rang out from the wooden doors. What good timing.

"…Lady Nive Maris and Lady Myullias Raiza have arrived," a voice said from beyond the doors. The staff member from just now, most likely.

Sharl looked to me for confirmation. I nodded once more.

"Open the doors, if you would."

With that, he stood up. I, too, followed his lead.

The door opened…and in stepped two women. Two surprisingly, breathtakingly beautiful women.

One had a head full of gray hair and sparkling, radiant red eyes. It was impossible to read her expression or her intent. The other had silver hair and eyes like amethyst. This woman had an almost ephemeral aura about her.

The two were probably a little younger than 20, or perhaps somewhere near 25. While I wasn't particularly skilled at determining the ages of women in general, I'd like to think that I had a rough idea.

I hardly went to such places now, but my adventuring seniors in the past would often bring me to certain taverns where women entertained guests at the tables. They'd often ask, "Oh, how old do you think I am?" and my guesses would often be far from the mark. As for my seniors, they managed to guess the entertainer's ages, only missing by two or three years. It was a strange feat they were capable of. How did they even know these things?

Well, that wasn't worth thinking about right now.

As the two women entered, the staff member exited the room, closing the doors behind him.

"Well met, Lady Nive, Lady Myullias. This individual before you is none other than the adventurer who slayed the tarasque, Sir…"

Sharl trailed off, turning to look at me, as if prompting me to introduce myself. Perhaps it was because he addressed the women in that way, but it was apparent to me that these two women were of high social standing.

What an unexpectedly empathetic merchant…

I introduced myself. "Rentt Vivie, Bronze-class adventurer, at your service."

I bowed my head. With that, I heard a voice respond somewhat unexpectedly.

"Ah, I don't really care for formalities like that! Raise your head, Mister Rentt. I'm not anyone special, not really... Ah. Hmm. Maybe Lady Myullias is special—important! Ah, no, no. I'm not important or special at all. While I do have a title, I'm more or less a normal citizen."

I slowly raised my head, somewhat cautiously, only to see one of the two women beaming.

From what I heard, the one who spoke was the gray-haired woman, Nive. In truth, I'd heard of her name before.

Nive Maris… That was none other than the name of a Gold-class adventurer from a neighboring land. She possessed an incredible amount of talent and ability, and she was said to be the Gold-class adventurer closest to a Platinum-class in terms of power. In recognition of her achievements and feats, she'd been granted the title of Baronetess. That was probably why she'd said those words.

As for her feats… Well. They were feats that didn't quite mesh very well with me at all…

"Yes. I, too, am an adventurer, and I've heard of your name. If I recall, you slayed a middle vampire that had established a nest in a large city. Vampire hunter…Nive Maris."

She was an adventurer who, for one reason or another, seemed to specialize in slaying vampires. Even so, most of her targets were lesser vampires, thralls, and the like. However, she'd once slain a middle vampire and its flock, weeding them out from the city they'd established themselves in. This act was what caused her name to spread far and wide.

While she was indeed strong, she also possessed abilities to seek out vampires who were walking among the living, hiding their form. I knew that much at least.

I did not, however, know of the means she employed to detect these vampires…

Whatever the case, it was undeniably true that she had crushed a middle vampire and its flock. She was truly capable of what the stories said, then.

Why did someone like this—a natural enemy of mine, even—show up here? Surely there were limits to how bad my luck could get?

I thought that from the bottom of my heart. I wanted to escape and leave right about now. I'd turn to her and say, "I apologize, but you are a vampire hunter, and I am a vampire. We cannot get along. Good day."

But of course I could do no such thing. The most I could do was speak to them and learn what they wanted, then naturally return home... I didn't see any other way out of this situation.

What would happen if my identity as a vampire was uncovered? It would be all over then. All I could do was fight as if my life depended on it, then escape to some other faraway land and reconstruct my life all over again. How would it turn out...?

I couldn't read the atmosphere at all. Nive looked...normal. If anything, she seemed very cheerful. I felt like I was gazing into an abyss I couldn't see the bottom of. And yet, she wasn't showing any signs of aggression or caution toward me... So had I not been found out? Which was it?

There was a young girl looking at me, nothing more. I felt like the distance could be closed between us instantly, and I could grab her by the collar and ask, "Which is it?!" But if I did that, I'd most certainly die.

I supposed there was nothing left to do but talk. If I were found out, I'd cross that bridge when I came to it.

"Oh, you know of me, I see. To think my name would spread to a rural place like this... Ah! I didn't mean to make fun of the place or anything, so you'll have to forgive me for that," Nive said, apologizing almost immediately for commenting on Maalt's geographical location.

While I didn't particularly care, there were some individuals who would be very displeased at such statements.

"What rural place? THIS. IS. A. CITY!" they would say.

It wasn't really much of a city, though... No matter how you spun it, Maalt really was just a small, rural town. Very rural. That was what I, Rentt Faina, who'd lived here for quite a long time, could say. It was an irrefutable truth. A reality.

"No. As you say, it is quite the rural place... What about that lady over there?"

I gestured toward the silver-haired woman. She was swift to respond.

"I apologize for my late introduction. I am saint Myullias Raiza, in service to the Church of Lobelia. Pleased to make your acquaintance."

She stared straight in my direction. Almost immediately, I felt a soft, strange sensation invade my body. It wasn't painful; it felt more like I'd been enveloped by an ambivalent feeling.

What...was this?

As I pondered, I could feel the divinity within me resonating, as if it were about to be pulled out of my very body itself. This was...

I turned to Myullias, who now had an expression of surprise on her face.

"Would you happen to be...blessed with divinity?" she asked.

I wanted to ask why she knew, but I already had my suspicions. I supposed I should keep up appearances in the meantime.

"That feeling just now... Was that you, by chance?"

"Yes, I thought to bless you with divinity... I am meant to cleave the darkness, you see... Um, how should I put this..."

Myullias quickly shot a glance at Nive. It seemed like she had difficulty explaining her actions. Nive, however, simply laughed at the gesture.

"Ah, no. Sorry about that. As you say, Mister Rentt, I'm quite famous, see? So, people try and off me all the time! If it was a normal attack or anything like that, I could deal with it, I'm sure, but I have to be careful about things like poisons, you know. That's why our saint, Lady Myullias, is here with us today... Well, more like I asked if she could come along and purify the surroundings. I can use divinity too, but things like cleansing and blessings... I'm no good with that stuff. Having an assistant from the Church of Lobelia is really helpful! I'm quite good at detecting vampires, you see. They're weak to divinity and all that, and if it's a weak one, just hit them with it, and poof! Off to the heavens they go."

Poof. To the heavens, Nive said.

Nive liked to talk, apparently. Although her words were casual and occasionally flippant, the contents were somewhat more important...

Myullias was a saint of the Church of Lobelia. For Nive to be able to request a personal escort in such a manner... I easily understood the amount of influence and power she wielded. And then there was that statement about her being good at her job...

But vampires being weak to divinity? I remained blessed with divinity, yet I seemed completely fine... Had I even heard of anything like that before? I didn't think so...

Was that really true? Well, you could channel it into your weapons and hurt a vampire with that... But hitting them with divinity alone? I'd never heard of anything like that. If that really were true, vampire hunting would be the monopolized territory of saints.

That was not the case however. Was that a lie then? This method didn't seem possible.

Perhaps Nive had picked up on my doubts.

"Well, it's not like there's completely no effect if you do it normally, you know? I have my ways, you see. Of finding out for certain. A very established methodology. I even discovered it too! That's why I can do it but others can't. That's all there is to it."

"A very established methodology, you say…"

Was there really such a thing? Other than what I instinctively knew of divinity and how to use it, I didn't have any other knowledge on the matter. As such, I couldn't gauge if such a thing was possible to begin with…

If anything, Nive was saying that only she could do it. Was this possible, even if she was well-versed in the ways of utilizing divinity…? I had no way of ascertaining the truth of her statements.

I glanced at Myullias, who was standing next to Nive. Her expression was one of muted suspicion, almost like she herself was saying, "Really? You can do that now?"

It seemed like these two women weren't exactly on good terms with each other. Nive may have asked for an assistant, but perhaps she didn't ask for Myullias specifically. Hmm.

"Yes, methodology!" Nive continued. "With this technique, I became a vampire hunter who never misses her mark! Of course, normal humans wouldn't feel a thing even if I did it to them. That is…if they're a normal human."

So…what exactly was all this supposed to mean? Was I found out? Or not? I couldn't make any judgments on my situation at all.

This…"methodology" of hers. Had she already done it? No, that couldn't be. If she'd already done it, I'd already be captured and in the process of being killed.

There was quite the famous saying about Nive Maris: her teeth and nails existed for the sole purpose of tearing vampires apart. So in that case, I guess I hadn't been found out yet?

Nevertheless, she suspected me. I understood that much. I also knew she was searching for information. In which case, would she be able to tell I was a vampire with this strange method of hers?

I continued wondering, worrying over the state of my secret.

"Oh, you doubt me? No, no. I get it. I do. No one believes me when I say it at first, you know? So this one time, I found a vampire walking around on the streets, and I tore them apart then and there... and everyone treated me like a murderer, see? But of course, the moment they realized the thing I'd killed was a vampire, a sizable reward was offered to me. Yeah...that was quite a disaster, wasn't it?"

Nive laughed. I could picture it in my mind now... It was a terrible sight.

But it went without saying that suddenly attacking a passerby on the street and tearing them apart would cause you to be treated as a murderer. From Nive's angle, though, not disposing of a vampire immediately upon spotting it was perhaps dangerous for the humans living in that particular place. Even so, to kill something in broad daylight, in full view of the citizenry... Of course they'd be treated as a murderer. If anything, they'd be immediately arrested.

Of course, an adventurer strong enough to hunt and kill vampires wouldn't be easily caught. If they were really innocent and had nothing to hide, however, chances were they'd cooperate with the authorities.

"So... Since it seems like you don't quite believe me, how about you try it? Just once? It's quite the rare experience, you know? How do I put it... It's kinda like a divine blessing? Almost? Sorta? Most of the time, normal humans are very happy when they see it! I suppose normal people are like that, huh? Divinity is a good thing; it brings blessings and happiness and the like, or so they think. And then you have religious groups that go about with their holy people and all that, but they don't bless people all that often! So that makes my job easier, see? Blessing people on the street. Oh, no, no. That isn't a criticism of the Church of Lobelia at all...yeah?"

Myullias's expression had been visibly darkening as Nive continued her lengthy monologue. You couldn't tell very well from a passing glance, but it was evident that Myullias was becoming less and less enthusiastic about her task.

Although Nive had denied it, her commentary was obviously a criticism of religious bodies and organizations. The Church of Lobelia, in particular, only gave out their blessings when their saints ventured out for one purpose or another. They were only in it for the money, I assumed, given how their whole holy water system worked.

In exchange for their relatively rare public appearances, the Church had quite a number of notably powerful practitioners of divinity. Was it because they were well paid?

To think the Church of the Eastern Sky got by on breadcrumbs and frugality... Well, that church had strong practitioners of divinity as well, proof that humans weren't always predisposed to evil.

"Try it, Lady Nive? You say that, but...it is quite frightening," I said, sheepishly.

The meaning behind my words was simple. *No! That's a bad idea! I would be in quite the bind!* But Nive didn't seem to understand this.

"Ah, sorry about that. You see, other people don't really trust me too often... Especially someone like me. 'Can we trust a flippant girl like that?' 'No, probably not.' Don't worry. I get it. Oh, how I get it... However. I do not spin tall tales about my own strength. Even so... hmmm. Ah! Mister Sharl. Care to try it out? I can see that interest on your face, hmmm?"

Nive suddenly directed her attention toward the merchant, who'd been standing and listening to us this entire time. He'd most likely been silent all this time out of consideration, not wanting to interrupt the conversation between her and myself.

To begin with, it was Nive who wanted to meet me. Perhaps he'd decided he shouldn't participate in the conversation unless the situation called for it.

Well, in this case, Nive spoke to him outright. Sharl, however, didn't have such an expression on his face at all. If anything, he looked slightly worried.

"Now, now! Think of it this way! You received a divine blessing! If you say that, wouldn't it be possible for such news to positively impact business? There are tangible benefits too, oh, yes! Monsters won't approach you for quite a while, you know! And, unlike the Church of Lobelia, I won't ask for any tithes or compensation! IT'S FREEEEEEEEEEEE! I do think it's quite the good deal, yeah?" Nive said, as if trying to sell a merchant his own wares.

Sharl didn't seem all too enthusiastic about this. Perhaps it was because he'd sensed that this would never end unless he agreed...

"...I understand. It really doesn't hurt, right?" Sharl spoke up, emphasizing the last half of his statement.

Nive nodded sagely. "Yes. If you aren't a vampire, that is. If you *are* a vampire, then it will hurt, oh, yes, it will hurt. But that's what it's for! You're...not a vampire, right?"

The sparkle returned to her eyes, right as she uttered that last bit.

Those were terrifying eyes. Eyes that pierced right to the bottom of my heart. There wasn't a single trace of the flippant nature that she'd been displaying up until now. Her words were no longer light, nor were they spoken in jest.

So this was the vampire hunter, Nive Maris...

Sharl swallowed for a moment as he noticed Nive's momentary expression. However, he quickly offered a response.

"But of course. I'd be lying if I said I didn't want to live forever, yes… But I don't think I would want to give up my humanity. Not if it means I end up a monster. If my life were to end, I would like to die as a human and peacefully depart with the blessings and forgiveness of the gods. Well…all things considered, I probably haven't lived a pious enough life to depart in such a fashion…" Sharl said, laughing bitterly.

What could I do? I sincerely apologize for becoming a monster, but it wasn't something I'd purposely done or sought out. If anything, I wanted to go back to being a human. So if I said something like that, I'd be safe, right?

Something in the direction of feeling your pride as a human. At least, that's what I thought, in my heart.

Nive soon responded.

"You are a merchant after all. To have a store as large as this, I'm sure many things have happened. But you know, I don't think the gods are that stingy, right? Surely they wouldn't condemn you to damnation because of a little…merchant activity. Right, Lady Myullias?"

Nive looked at her companion. Myullias regarded her with a mix of incredulity and curiosity. Maybe Myullias didn't know if Nive truly believed what she said.

With a vague expression, Myullias replied, "I cannot possibly fathom the will of the gods. All I know is that the gods would not discriminate. All those who wish for salvation will be saved."

"See? There you have it," Nive said offhandedly.

Sharl merely continued laughing awkwardly, seemingly more relaxed about his fate.

"Well, then, Lady Nive... If you would. As you said just now, you don't mind if I use it in my advertising? That I, Sharl Stheno, have received a divine blessing from vampire hunter, Lady Nive Maris..."

Given the nature of Sharl's question, I could assume that few knew of Nive having reserves of divinity. "Were you not hiding it?" would be the true nature of his question.

Nive, on the other hand...

"Oh, I don't mind at all. I wasn't hiding it anyway, see. Those who know will know. So, since I have your consent, I'll do it now, okay?"

"Ah, yes. Please."

With that, Sharl got on his knees, kneeling before Nive.

That posture was the same one adopted by devotees of the Church of Lobelia, the correct way in which you were to receive a divine blessing.

Intermission: Myullias Raiza, Saint

After Sharl positioned himself, kneeling appropriately, Nive held out her hand and placed it some distance above the merchant's head. Her fingers were cupped, as if she'd intended to scoop something up with them.

I could see traces of divinity faintly gathering in her palm.

While mana was invisible to the naked eye, divinity was a little different. So long as you concentrated, you could make it out, ever so slightly. It was all but impossible to discern from a distance, of course, but it was hardly an issue with me this close.

Even so, I was witnessing quite the concentrated mass of divinity. My reserves would have already dried up had I tried to emulate such a thing.

Although Nive Maris held the title of Baronetess, she was, at the end of the day, an adventurer. It was surprising to see someone with such huge reserves of divinity run about in the wild in such a fashion. Under normal circumstances, individuals who possessed that much divinity would have long since received invitations from religious bodies or holy knight orders. Such organizations would have bent over backward to invite such talented persons into their ranks.

That in mind, I supposed Nive had some sort of personal agenda. Vampire hunting most likely, judging by all I'd observed thus far.

There was a soft, audible pop, and a small, flicking flame soon appeared in Nive's cupped hands. It was not a normal flame by any means. Glowing softly, it was an incandescent white. What a mysterious flame…

I, however, knew that the flame itself was a coagulation of divinity.

"Holy Fire, see? Even among practitioners of divinity, only those who are blessed with great reserves, and are well-trained in its use, can materialize it. A sort of holy flame that dwells within oneself, you see."

Myullias, who'd been spectating from the side, regarded the flame with a most mystified and curious expression.

"Why would you use such a thing to discern vampires from normal townsfolk…?"

While Nive claimed that her technique was unique to her alone, Myullias's inquiry suggested there were many others who were capable of the same thing.

Myullias continued. "Those who receive the blessings of the Holy Fire often manifest unique abilities, based on one's disposition. The ways in which it can be used are countless. I suppose Lady Nive's Holy Fire has been specialized to detect vampires… Such is a possibility…"

She seemed to refuse making any concrete declarations.

Would I be able to use the same thing if I worked hard toward such a goal? Would I be able to gain some sort of special power from it then? For some reason, I felt my abilities would mostly be limited to the creation or enrichment of plant fertilizer…

I turned to Myullias. "Do you wield such a flame as well, Lady Myullias?"

"It is all but impossible for me... I lack the sheer amount of divinity for such a thing, nor do I have the skill and technique to do so."

"How many in the Church of Lobelia are capable of such, then...?"

"That... I do apologize, but it is not something I have the privilege of divulging to outsiders," Myullias said, slightly troubled.

She made it clear that I shouldn't have asked that.

Still, she continued on. "I make no references to the church on this matter, but in general, few practitioners of divinity are known to have this level of skill. A typical organization would have perhaps... two, three individuals. As far as I understand."

She most likely included the church in her list of "typical organizations." A bare-bones but functional explanation.

From what I'd heard of Nive and her exploits, I'd imagined her to be quite the rigid person. Unexpectedly, Nive was hardly the religious sort.

Now that I thought about it... Nive wasn't very religious at all, but the little snide remarks she had for the church and similar organizations would be enough to annoy anyone. Then there was the issue of how she said it...

As I continued my inner monologue, the white flame in Nive's palms grew to an astonishing size. It had now stretched all the way to the ceiling, the flames just centimeters short of licking the building. If Sharl could see this, I was sure he'd be surprised. Fortunately for him, his eyes were closed, and I supposed that was his salvation in the matter. After all, anyone would assume having such a huge flame placed on their head would be nothing short of fatal.

Despite the presence of such a blatant tower of flame, the room didn't feel hot or stuffy. I didn't even feel anything from where I stood. I couldn't feel any heat at all.

When I looked up at the ceiling, it looked like flames were ravaging the beams, but I couldn't discern any burn marks or damage. I supposed this Holy Fire of hers was different than the normal fire I was accustomed to, on some fundamental level.

Soon enough, Nive began parting her cupped hands. Almost like a silent stream of water, the Holy Fire fell upon the merchant, drops of luminous white trickling down onto his being.

Fire! Sharl is going to catch fire!

Instead, Sharl was briefly illuminated as the flames wrapped around him, slowly enveloping his being...before quietly disappearing altogether.

Again and again the drops fell, this scene repeating itself. Eventually, the pool in Nive's hands ran dry, and a strange silence filled the room, as if nothing had ever happened in the first place.

"So! It seems like Sharl here isn't a vampire at all! Well, then! Next!" Nive practically shouted as her eyes met with mine.

At that, Sharl opened his eyes and heaved an audible sigh of relief.

But why was she talking about it as if this were some sort of assembly line?

While that's what I wanted to say to Nive Maris, vampire hunter, she was hardly a person I could argue with. Regardless, I wasn't able to risk undergoing the same process as Sharl.

What should I do?

Was there a means of escape...?

Ah... There was something.

"From what you mentioned just now, Lady Nive, monsters don't approach someone if they receive such a blessing, right?"

"Hmm… I suppose not…"

"Well, then, I'm an adventurer. Not being able to encounter monsters would be problematic, so I'll respectfully decline…"

A great excuse, Rentt, I thought. Nive however…

"Ah, don't you worry about that. I can leave that specific part of it out, see. No problem at all."

A swift response…

I'd tried my best to communicate my reluctance, but it seemed like Nive was having none of it. But I wasn't going to back down so easily, either.

"Perhaps if I'd gone first, there'd be no issue, but having seen that… Well, I feel I'm not quite brave enough to accept this blessing…"

It wasn't a strange excuse. Even if they were told it was entirely safe, there was no man in these lands who wouldn't fear being burnt by what seemed to be fire—and nothing *but* fire.

But Nive…

"I understand how you feel… Hmm. Maybe it's just me? Mister Rentt…you've been kinda shifty just now, haven't you? A little avoidant too… Perhaps you feel unwell?" Nive said, tilting her head ever so slightly. That familiar glimmer was back in her eyes. She had that same look when interrogating Sharl on the possibilities of him being a vampire.

I could hear myself mentally gulping, swallowing hard. The sound reverberated in my mind. I didn't let it show on my face.

Calmly…

"I've no intention of avoiding it. It's just that…I'm scared, you know? Of that fire, I mean. That's all there is to it."

Scared that I'd be found out, more like. But I couldn't say that, so I made some excuse about being afraid of fire.

Nive, as if convinced, slowly nodded her head. "Well, it's not all that scary, you know? Well, then... Hmm. I guess I'll give up on it for today...but not really. ALL RIGHT, THEN! Let's go!"

With that, she raised an arm in my direction, tendrils of white flame shooting out from them faster than the eye could see. All of those tendrils were aimed at none other than myself.

This was bad. I had to dodge them, but... As expected of a Gold-class adventurer, her aim was true. It was beyond good—not a single one of Nive's flames missed. I could only cry internally at my lack of ability and skill.

Despite all the strength and benefits my current state gave me, I was still insignificant compared to a Gold-class adventurer who was on the cusp of achieving Platinum-class.

But of course, the entire kneeling affair with Sharl would be all but impossible on a typical passerby. I felt myself convinced despite the entire situation that Nive had other means of delivering her flames.

I wondered for a moment what I was doing, feeling impressed and ponderous in such a life-and-death situation. I was burning, burning up. White, flickering flames licked every inch of my body. My entire body was now enveloped by these flames, just as I'd seen moments ago with Sharl.

Would Nive find out that I was a vampire, based on this ability of hers? Many people would surely be troubled at such a revelation...

A flurry and vortex of emotions raced through my mind.

Then...

"...Huh. It...isn't much. Actually, it's not very hot at all..."

Strangely, *unexpectedly*, nothing out of the ordinary happened. Perhaps I just felt that way, but as far as I could see, there didn't seem to be anything amiss with me, despite the flames.

Did this mean…I passed?

I felt a momentary flash of elation, like I'd just won some bet.

But I should have already known that these flames didn't feel hot in the slightest, especially after observing Sharl. Turning my mind back to the fire, it was a strange sensation indeed. If I had to put it into words, it felt like the flames were tickling me. They seemed to be poking around my insides, exploring me all over.

Relieved there were no evident problems, I began enjoying the feeling. It felt like the divinity in me had become more vibrant, more alive, as well.

Was I just imagining things? It wouldn't be too terrible a thing to stay like this for a while... It was much akin to the sensation you felt when entering a hot bath.

But I couldn't just stand here forever. After a while, the sensation of being kneaded and occasionally poked from within my body slowly disappeared. The flames, too, ebbed soon after.

With the white flames now completely gone, and Nive having conducted some sort of inspection, she stared straight at me, before loudly announcing...

"I see you aren't a vampire either, Mister Rentt!"

No, I am *a vampire!*

I wanted so badly to point this out to Nive, but I let it slide for now. Oh, how I very much wanted to point this out to her, even if death itself would be waiting for me as soon as I said those words...

But luckily, such events did not come to pass.

"Hmm... Pardon me for asking, but...what just happened? All I saw was Sir Rentt suddenly panicking and moving in a strange way..." Sharl said, his expression grim.

Me? Panicking? Strange movements?

Well...no. Not really. Come now. Who wouldn't panic at the prospect of being burned alive by a strange flame? It wasn't anything to run from, given Sharl's perspective of the entire affair...

"Mister Rentt here can see the blessing of divinity, you see? So he tried to dodge it."

Nive was quick to offer an explanation, as usual.

In other words, I assumed Sharl was unable to see it. Not even that gigantic Holy Fire on his head?

As I continued wondering about all this, Nive chose to busy herself by giving Sharl an in-depth explanation. Approaching me, Myullias leaned in subtly, softly whispering into my ear.

"Mister Rentt. Holy Fire is divinity given shape. Those who haven't been blessed with divinity are incapable of perceiving it. But of course, it's possible to make divinity visible, but if one doesn't purposely do that, it usually cannot be seen by the naked eye. As such, to Mister Sharl, you were dancing in place on your own with no provocation whatsoever. At least, that's how he would have seen it."

A stunning description of events. Stunning, with regards to the segment where I began dancing for no reason whatsoever.

To think that Holy Fire would be invisible to those not blessed by divinity... I supposed it made sense, considering how mana worked. Some people could see mana outright, while others could not. Most mages and the like were unable to perceive it as well. There were also exceptions like Lorraine and her especially perceptive eyes.

More importantly, the fact that I'd been seen as some sort of strange eccentric was probably the saddest part of this entire affair.

"...Well. With that, Misters Sharl, Rentt. You both aren't vampires, and are no longer under any suspicion! Thank you for your kind cooperation," Nive said, wrapping up her explanation to the merchant.

Nive had most likely explained that divinity was invisible, and events ended with both of us harmlessly blessed without any issues, and that was that.

Sharl was one thing, but did I really cooperate? Hmm...

My discontent had somehow become apparent to Nive. She shook her head before responding in a somewhat indignant tone.

"What are you gonna have me do about it? After all, I'd heard nothing about you having been blessed with divinity, Mister Rentt. Not until I got here anyway. Honestly, all I wanted to do was sneakily use my Holy Fire to see if any of you were vampires, then go home without saying a thing. Of course, I intended to eliminate any vampires if we did find them, you see. No vampires were harmed in our little outing, no doubt due to me not having done enough scouting beforehand, yes. But…you're at fault too, you know? To have such special skills as an adventurer, and not go about using them… Yeah."

Such was Nive's one-sided declaration.

How terrible for her to say! She herself was the most irregular one here, yet she was framing that entire encounter as my fault.

Most adventurers who were blessed with divinity didn't command it at a level where it could be used practically. If they did have such reserves and skill, they'd already have made it into the rank of some holy knight order ages ago. From what I understood, they paid well, and your social standing would be greatly improved.

But if I had no divinity, and didn't notice her flames…would that mean Nive could have easily detected me from the get-go and suddenly plunged a stake of some sort into my heart?

Ah…truly. It was truly a blessing that I'd gone out of my way to fix up that rickety shrine… I really should go back and clean that place up once in a while… I had been saved because of the divinity within me after all.

At least, I felt that way.

It was precisely because Nive was able to do this that she was able to detect vampires hidden among normal townsfolk. I should've given it more thought to begin with.

Even if this were Nive Maris we were talking about, suddenly setting people on fire in the street, while claiming to be searching for vampires, wouldn't exactly come across as sane reasoning.

Though in truth, that's exactly what she did…

I pictured her setting people on fire, laughing all the while as she did it. A vivid image in my mind… How fitting.

Hmm… I was possibly being a little too biased here. I hadn't even known this woman for an hour. Half of all this was due to Nive's terrible personality, though. I'd said I didn't wish to undergo this vampire testing, but she'd gone and done it anyway.

"Hmm… I don't quite understand, but are you telling me, and correct me if I'm wrong, that Lady Nive willfully acted in such a way that would cause Sir Rentt to think he was in danger?" Sharl inquired.

Slight hints of anger could be observed on the merchant's face. What was Sharl angry about…? I didn't quite understand, tilting my head.

"As long as you two aren't vampires," Nive spoke up, "there are no problems. I had no intention of harming anyone in the first place. But see, looking at Mister Rentt's reaction, I kinda had a feeling, and it played out like it did. I'll apologize to the both of you for that… Especially you, Mister Sharl. For asking all that of you."

What was all this about? But before I could ponder, Myullias was quick to add on to Nive's explanation.

"If I may say so, I was most likely brought along as a means of utilizing the radiance of the Church of Lobelia. To a merchant, the church is… It is a little difficult for me to say, but it is almost impossible to defy the church, if I could put it that way. While the Church of Lobelia doesn't have much influence here in Yaaran, it is a large religious organization, with roots all across the lands. There are many within the ranks of the church's followers.

If certain maneuvers are carried out, it would surely be difficult for a merchant involved in business between kingdoms, such as Mister Sharl. It wouldn't be difficult for the church to bring about such events if it so desired."

Nive seemed genuinely impressed at Myullias' explanation.

"To think Lady Myullias would provide such an explanation, hmm-hmm! I thought you were the type who lived and died by the teachings of Lobelia..."

Nive then quickly turned to me. "So, that's how it is, see? Don't blame Mister Sharl too much. He actually did a ton to prevent me from meeting you, Rentt! When I made the request, he had this explanation and that explanation. He'd skirt the issue at any chance. I was at my wit's end... So I called in some favors at the Church of Lobelia, see? Asked them for help and all that. I also promised him that I wouldn't do anything to put you in danger, or hurt you. On top of that, I actually really did wanna meet with you, Mister Rentt. It's true! If you really were a vampire, I would have eliminated you quietly, in some place where no eyes would reach, see.

"Well, since I've explained all this, I may as well let you in on this little secret. Mister Sharl here actually did feel that something was off, you know? I'm famous, after all. As such, he wouldn't allow just me to meet with you, Rentt. That's why he's here too, yes? In other words, Sharl, as the head of the Stheno Company, wanted to be here to protect his client, even if it meant he may be exposed to danger, as well. Quite the nice guy, no? Unlike how he looks."

How...unexpected.

Sharl had quite the strict, severe look about him. Even so, he seemed accommodating, and empathetic expressions frequently showed upon his face. I'd thought this was all a front, and that he was actually a scheming, plotting merchant, but reality was somewhat different. If anything, Sharl was a good and just merchant.

Was that why his company did so well?

Come to think of it, the sales floors below did feature a wide range of goods, of respectable quality no less. Stores that just wanted to earn a quick sum of coin would most likely have a smaller inventory. The fact that the Stheno Company didn't do this suggested it was instead built off hard work and honest trade.

I glanced at Sharl. While he looked like a merchant with ulterior motives, said face of his was now apologetic, even remorseful.

"...Is what this person says true?" I asked.

"...It is. I... There was nothing more I could do. If it were just an affair involving me, maybe I could have come up with something. But to use the store as a shield... I... I have staff members! And they all have families! I have a duty to protect this store, this company of ours. However, we have a duty to protect our customers, as well. That...is why I am here," Sharl replied, affirming the situation at hand.

There were no problems so long as I wasn't perceived to be a vampire. There was no reason for Sharl to go this far, was what I felt. It seemed he had his pride as a merchant, hence his actions.

Faced with those choices, Sharl offered me up as a sacrifice of sorts. That was one way to put it. While we both ended up on the proverbial chopping block, it seemed he felt bad for dragging me into all this, which was most likely why he'd offered me all those concessions at the start of our meeting...

All that investigating into my background, as well. Had Sharl noticed that something was off about my origins and had done so with the intent of preparing himself for what may occur after the meeting...?

Ah, but it'd be quite funny if he were making plans for a culturally-accurate funeral. I *was* already dead.

...Not a very good joke, Rentt Faina...

Perhaps Sharl was concerned about the possibility of me having a family, and had intended to inform them of my fate should anything occur. Nothing more than a deduction of mine, of course, but looking at Sharl as he was now, I wouldn't be surprised if he were to do such a thing.

Then I considered that the merchant himself could have very well lost his life had he taken a single wrong step... I had a feeling that Nive didn't have a shred of forgiveness in her for vampire sympathizers, not even for a moment. I could feel the intensity of her hatred from the way she'd been directing these questions, and how she'd gone about the entire affair.

But to think she would go and tell me all this...

I looked straight at Nive, and questioned her bluntly.

"I think I have a grasp of the situation. For some reason, you had severe suspicions of me, that I was a vampire of some sort. Although I didn't exactly cooperate with you, my innocence has been proven. Now, may I ask if there was some reason for, well, all this?"

That was what her method of discerning vampires claimed. It was wrong, of course.

Although the situation ended with an outcome that was in my favor, I wanted to know the reasons for Nive's suspicions, if there were any. If I didn't discover that here and now, something else might happen further down the road.

Then there was the issue of my bad luck knowing no bounds... I wouldn't want to make any fatal mistakes just because I'd forgotten to affirm even one detail.

"Oh, sure. I suppose you have a right to know. In addition, I also have a little request of my own. You remember how Mister Sharl said I sought adventurers of certain capabilities, yes? That, you see, wasn't entirely a lie..."

"So…I'm sure you've heard the stories recently? Of adventurers disappearing in dungeons, yeah?"

Nive's explanation began with such a statement.

Where had I heard this before, I wondered. Ah, yes. There was that incident, quite some time ago…

"Is this perhaps about the newly registered adventurers who have gone missing? Quite a few of them at that."

Nive nodded. "Yes, that. Exactly that. From what I can tell, this is clearly the work…of vampires."

A sudden declaration of the culprit. As far as I understood, the guild was searching for the perpetrator even now…but had had no luck so far. That's what Sheila had told me…but what if the guild had made some discoveries?

Were vampires truly the cause? Even if that were true, I was by no means a criminal.

"Would that not be too broad of an assumption, Lady Nive? After all, no desiccated adventurer corpses were found. How did you come to such a conclusion?"

An impossible, implausible conclusion, I wanted to say. Nive, however, withdrew a map from a magic bag on her belt and spread it open on a table near us. Various bits of information were jotted down on the map, details here and there sporadically.

Upon closer inspection, I realized all these notations had something to do with vampires. Details on the year, month, and day of encounters, the types of vampire, the amount, if they'd been slain…or were still alive. Countless notations filled the parchment.

To think she would possess so much information… She'd done a good job gathering it, at least.

A single look at the map was enough to convince me of one thing: Nive's passion toward exterminating vampires.

Even so, I still wasn't very fond of the woman…but it was worth hearing her out.

Nive pointed out a certain kingdom in the west, and continued her explanation.

"This place… A town by the name of Ruguella. In this very town, about half a year ago, a certain incident occurred, you see. Newly registered adventurers went missing."

"What about it?"

While not exactly a common occurrence, it wasn't unheard of either. If anything, new adventurers often lost their lives due to their recklessness and lack of knowledge. As such, no matter where these events occurred, they were never anything to pay too much heed to.

Nive, however, pressed on, moving her finger slightly to the east.

"Next is this place. A town called Oradoras. Adventurers went missing there too. New ones, yeah?"

Continuing on with her explanation, she moved her finger east again and again, tracing a path through about roughly 30 towns and cities, all having faced the same issue. Lastly, her finger stopped on a familiar place: Maalt.

The string of adventurer disappearances traced a neat line east, straight from Ruguella to Maalt.

This…

Nive was already aware that I'd picked up on the pattern.

"As you can see, these disappearances, for some strange reason, keep going east. And then, at last, it made its way to Maalt…and that much was fine."

"Right…"

"But of course, you're probably thinking that just this alone isn't enough to claim that the entire affair is the work of vampires. To begin with, of these 30 incidents, 11 towns and cities chose not to announce or make the public aware of them. Perhaps that isn't an accurate way of putting it... Adventurers die, right? In dungeons and all that, so them disappearing was simply seen as that. I affirmed all these missing persons cases myself, and can attest to their validity. Looking at all this, I sensed something was amiss. I had a gut feeling that vampires were involved. There was no mistaking it."

That... What was I to make of that? Perhaps those adventurers really had lost their lives in the dungeon.

To begin with, people dying in dungeons was sad and unfortunate, yes, but nothing to write home about. This applied doubly to newer adventurers, as their fatality rate and frequency was somewhat higher. Even if there was a slightly higher number of fatalities, you could reasonably assume they'd simply delved too deep, overestimating their prowess.

Realistically speaking, such was possible enough. As such, I queried Nive on this point.

"The adventurer's guild often sees this as a regular occurrence, however. The guild doesn't see it as a big issue, right?"

"There is that, yes. However, I discovered that the guilds have found out certain things, you see. They simply kept these discoveries a secret. In fact, a number of thralls were found in those towns, and were hunted and destroyed, of course. Once you get to Gold-class, there are certain records you can access in the adventurer guild's documents, you see? So, here's the thing... While there are some records on slain vampires in those ledgers, strangely enough, no records of those slain thralls could be found. As you know, thralls are the familiars, underlings, of vampires. If vampires didn't exist, thralls wouldn't either. To add on to all that, here's the kicker. See, the appearance of those thralls and their equipment, right? None other than the newly registered adventurers who had gone missing. And that's that."

I felt that the adventurer's guild had gravely sinned for keeping all this information secret… But then again, I supposed that's what they would do.

Nive, as if reading my mind, continued on. "Yeah… If you know that much, then you'd understand why the guild said nothing too. After all, if the existence of thralls was affirmed, tons of adventurers would gather at those towns. For a time, the town would have a boom in business, but this influx of adventurers would only take jobs away from the local ones, and they'd just be left sitting around, even though they were the ones usually offering their services to the guild. So of course the guilds would say nothing."

Quite the terrible affair, that, but then again, the adventurer's guild was by no means a noble or entirely morally upright organization. Maalt's guild operated on somewhat cleaner ethics, yes, but such wasn't necessarily true for other towns. The guilds of those towns decided their own culture.

Guilds that were disliked, those that abused their power, guilds that had little to no influence and power at all… There were all sorts. Adventurer's guilds were more or less gatherings of ruffians and the like, so I supposed that could hardly be avoided. Even so, the fact that all guilds maintained some capability to offer a service was something quite admirable…or was it?

Please go about your tasks properly, adventurer's guilds of the world…

But from what Nive said, thralls created from newly registered adventurers had been witnessed by multiple individuals. If that were indeed true…

Nive went on, pacing around as she did so.

"I'm sure you can tell from everything you've seen up until this point, but I'm always searching for vampires, see. If I ever see anything strange, I often go and check out the situation myself. There were many duds of course... But this time, I'm right on the mark. As such, I've been advancing east as well, keeping an eye out for any thralls in each of these towns and cities. As fate would have it, I found them in many of these places. Eliminated the moment I found them, yeah? And so, at the end of the trail, I'm here for their head. The big boss. I came all the way here, but I can't find them. Nothing, not even now. But they must be here, somewhere, so..."

"Is there not the possibility that this vampire has already left Maalt?"

It was, after all, a vampire that continuously headed east. There was a possibility it was no longer in this town at all.

Nive nodded.

"Yes, but I can't be sure of it. However, in my experience, a vampire who has hunted this many humans won't just stop. No, it can't stop. Given the cases of newly registered adventurers strangely disappearing, it should still be here, in this town. If it's not, then missing persons cases should be popping up all over the place. Somewhere else, that is.

"According to my sources, these incidents haven't occurred in surrounding towns yet, so, it must still be here."

It seemed Nive had quite a fair amount of sources. As for her means, well... I'd heard that Gold-class adventurers were able to use part of the guilds' information network, so it was probably something along those lines. Or perhaps it was Nive's personal network...

I didn't really know if this was true, but I had a feeling her claims were most likely correct.

However…

"Well, then…why suspect me?" I asked.

Was I that strange?

"I came to this town searching for a vampire," Nive answered me swiftly. "Well. You know, people in this town are all kinda weird, but among them, see, there's this one person who's really weird. It's none other than you, Mister Rentt. You came to this town recently, got promoted to Bronze-class in a short amount of time, and put down a tarasque all by yourself. I think you get what I'm saying, don't you? It's not impossible, yes, but new adventurers who are capable of such a thing? Very rare. However, if you were a vampire, then such feats would hardly be beyond you. On top of that, you're only active during hours where there is little activity in the town, in the streets. A common behavior among vampires, right? They avoid coming into contact with humans and hardly venture out during the day. Your mask, robe, the paleness of your skin… If you think of how your mask could be used to hide the fangs in your mouth… So. The more I looked at you, the stranger you became… But it would seem I was mistaken, so I'll have to apologize."

Well, I was convinced. Nive was right. All of it! She really had done her research and had specifically targeted me. I now understood why she carried the title of vampire hunter.

Myullias and Sharl, too, seemed convinced at the explanation Nive offered.

But now I had the affirmation that I wasn't a vampire—to Nive, at least. With all that had happened, I had a good mind to ask for a fair amount of compensation on my part.

Which is why I said, "I apologize for my strange appearance, but to think you would suspect me of such because of it…"

"Ah, yeah. There's that. Terrible, isn't it? Terrible affair. I understand. Not something I say often, but I understand. But see, that was also sorta why I offered to purchase the tarasque materials at such a high price, you see. As a kind of apology for all this, you know? And then there's this. You probably don't need it, but…"

Nive detached something from the detailed map that she had unfurled on the table, turning and handing the mystery item to me. Some sort of paper…? On it was written a registration number. Judging from the format, it was one of the guild's.

If I had this document, I'd be able to hand it over to guild staff, who'd most likely put me in touch with Nive. It was a strange means of communication, as the speed of contact depended on where the individual was and how long it took to find them… This was especially true for individuals like Nive, who seemed everywhere but nowhere at once. Contacting her would be extremely difficult.

"Come on, don't make such a face! Maybe you'll need it one day."

"I think such a possibility would be quite low…"

If possible, I didn't want anything more to do with this woman.

"See, Mister Rentt. I really like investigating things and all that… But more importantly, my gut feeling is…important? You know. I feel that way pretty often. So by my gut feeling, I'd say… Mister Rentt. Someday. You'll need. To contact me. With. This," Nive replied ominously.

I could almost feel a violent, blunt force behind each of her uttered words. *Please, vampire hunter. Leave me be already…*

Though Nive's gut feeling was quite accurate, if I could say so myself. After all, she'd correctly discerned my identity as a vampire based on that alone.

But saying I'd need to contact her in the future? How ominous…

Whatever the case, I should take it with me. I made a mental note to ask Lorraine to give the piece of paper a once over, in the event that there was any kind of magic or enchantment inscribed within…

"Well, then. Should we get to the actual topic for today?" Nive said.

Momentarily, I couldn't help but question myself: what was the topic again…?

Ah, yes, I remember. The sale of the tarasque ingredients.

The sale had come with many additional conditions and clauses. I wondered just how much it would all fetch.

With all these new objects of desire appearing recently, I found myself hungering for coin. You could never have too much coin. For instance, there was the equipment that could be forged from the earth dragon-tinged mana iron, a larger magic bag than the one I had now…

"So you did wish to purchase the items after all? Surprising."

The sale of the items could have all been a ruse for calling me to this place. But it seemed I was mistaken.

Nive was quick to respond. "Sure, sure, I'll buy it all right. A normal transaction and all that. Tarasque parts are worth their weight in some precious metal or other, you know? Especially the poison glands, see. It works especially well against vampires."

"Tarasque poison is effective against vampires…?"

"It's not a well-known fact, yeah? Vampires have a high resistance to poisons and everything, but a tarasque's is surprisingly effective. In fact, the poison in question is enough to paralyze lesser vampires. As for the greater ones, well… It's less of an effect, sure, but if I had a choice, I'd much rather have them plastered with it. So, the poison glands of a tarasque. A necessity for vampire hunters like me, really."

But the poison had no effect on me. If the Holy Fire incident a few moments ago was anything to go by, I was significantly different from the typical vampire. I even had doubts about what I was from the very start, vampire or not.

My current state defied most forms of classification. In the end, Lorraine and I could only come to our best conclusions given what data we had. That was why I'd been classified as a type of vampire in the first place. We probably had no other means of furthering this research…

We *could* always ask for the favor of the gods, for one, but that would be difficult in many ways to say the least. To go to a temple of any kind with this body of mine, a certain degree of courage was needed. Not that I had that right now, but I supposed I'd eventually have to go regardless…

Well, that was that. Nothing could be done about it now, and this was hardly something I should be thinking about at this point in time.

More importantly: the value of the tarasque parts.

"For an adventurer such as yourself, Lady Nive, surely hunting a tarasque or two wouldn't be much of an issue."

The materials were expensive, but surely that wouldn't be the case if you were as strong as Nive. That, in turn, could lower the perceived value of the materials, hence my question, partially asked out of worry.

But Nive…

"I could hunt it if I wanted to, I suppose. But see, when it comes to tarasques, no matter where they live, really, they all live in those swamps, yeah? The preparations take forever, and if I had the time to be doing that I should be hunting vampires instead. Fortunately, some adventurers who do hunt them come by every now and then... If anything, Mister Rentt, looks like you go there pretty often, huh?"

She asked this.

While tarasques lived in a variety of locations across the lands, the poisons they secreted eventually ended up turning their habitat into a noxious pit of poison, much like the Tarasque Swamp itself. As such, no matter where you searched for the beasts, it was almost a given that you would have to cross such terrain. It wasn't difficult to see why Nive would find that troublesome.

I supposed even an adventurer like Nive strongly preferred to not get mired in mud, poison, and grime.

As for me... I didn't go about doing it just because I liked to.

However...

"A few reasons compel me to return to the swamp... A certain material I must harvest, you see. So..."

"Hmm..." Nive paused momentarily, giving my words some thought. "A material you have to harvest in the swamp, you say...? So this material would most likely be...Dragon Blood Blossoms, the noxious swamp bird, or...the tarasque's poison gem. One of these, I suppose. I see..."

I was careful not to spill any more hints than necessary, but, for some reason, Nive was already able to pick up on all that. Myullias, too, seemed surprised.

"Your expressions and demeanor haven't changed in the slightest, however....."

Such was Myullias's analysis of the situation. But it was no good. Nive had already extracted the information she needed... I still had a long ways to go.

"Well, then! Pleasantries and other kinds of gossip aside, I guess we should talk business. Mister Sharl, if you would be so kind. How much was the tarasque going for at the auction again?"

"Yes," Sharl nodded, recounting the information. "On that matter, tarasque parts usually differ in price, depending on the region of the monster. I could give an approximation... On average, the parts would cost anywhere between 60 gold pieces, to perhaps 200. However, the carcass has been well-preserved this time around due to how it was slain. All the relevant parts are in good condition. At the very least, the auction would have started from a hundred gold pieces. The rest would be luck, and how far the bidders go. Judging by the individuals present at the slated auction, however, the price would rise above 300 gold pieces or more. That is my humble estimate."

Hmm... The more I listened to Sharl go on, the more I realized such monetary values were far beyond the reach of normal citizens such as myself. Yes, a tarasque was a large creature, and many materials could be collected from its carcass, and the individual components could be easily priced, but... I supposed this particular product didn't enter the market very often, circumstances being what they were...

"I see. In that case, the original agreement was for me to pay twice the final bidding price. So let's start from the assumption doubling that would amount to about 600 gold pieces, yeah? Well, there's always the possibility of auction maniacs driving up the price. So it may very well go to four, say, five hundred gold pieces before it goes under the hammer," Nive declared.

Sharl, however, responded with a somewhat worried expression.

"Yes… Yes, I suppose you could say that. It is a rare occurrence, but buyers can often misread the competition. Sometimes someone raises the bid by ten gold pieces, and another does so by a hundred, only to regret it immediately after. But something like that would only happen once. As such, I guess it is realistic to say that the final auction price would not exceed 400 gold pieces."

"Well, then. Twice that is 800 pieces, yeah? And then…a token of goodwill from me, if I may say so. Under normal circumstances, how much compensation would be paid to a common citizen if their life were endangered for no good reason?"

"I would say…ten to fifty gold pieces. Such is the case with most of these scenarios. There is the consideration of occupation, as well. But even if, say, *I* were to be killed, the compensation would most likely not exceed 50 gold pieces."

What Sharl spoke of was something known even to me. The lives of common citizenry were cheap to say the least.

But so long as you had ten gold pieces, you'd surely be able to live a relatively stable life, even if you lost the breadwinner of the family. It was a reasonably functional sum.

However, in the township of Maalt, even the life of Sharl, the head of a large trading company, would only be worth 50 gold pieces. In my case…the amount would be much lower. I was just a nameless adventurer; I couldn't even be certain about my tomorrows. My life may even be cheaper than that of the common citizenry.

Despite that, the price of a life is usually determined by the local ruling lords and ladies of a region. Under normal circumstances, so long as two individuals were of similar standing in society, even their professions wouldn't serve to alter this sum by much.

But of course, the social impact of deaths could differ. If Sharl were to lose his life, and myself soon after, I supposed the difference would be quite large. But I never gave the matter much thought.

This would all change if the one who'd passed on was a noble of some kind, but I supposed that was a topic for another time.

"Now, then," Nive continued on. "Let us set the compensation for Mister Rentt's hypothetical loss of life to 50 gold pieces. I did try to do something like that, after all. Even if it all ended without incident, the fact I lied and did my fair bit of cheating probably doesn't change much, yeah? So let's add that to the whole compensation affair as well…"

In other words, Nive was proposing she would give me a hundred gold pieces for my trouble.

That was…expensive! However, if I thought about it another way, I could kill any amount of tarasques from here on out, yet each attempt may very well end with me losing my life. The possibility was there, so I supposed that was…fair. In its own way.

Again, this was all up to the ruling nobles of the region. While there were some unexpected situations thrown into the mix, it seemed part of it was the work of Nive's conscience.

"Would the total be 900 gold pieces then?"

Hmm… If I really did get that much, I'd be able to obtain everything I wanted. A bigger magic bag would cause half of that to vanish, of course, while the rest could go into equipment, weapons, and the like…

Magic bags were unreasonably expensive…

Even if I should spend such a sum, all I'd be able to afford was a bag with three times the capacity of my current one.

As for a pouch or bag that could contain a tarasque… I did see one at an auction prior, but the asking price was a 1,800 gold pieces, maybe a little more. That was double what I'd be receiving, so purchasing that was all but impossible.

I wasn't dissatisfied at Nive's offer by any means. If anything, I was troubled by what to do with all this coin. Should I save for another bag? Or use what I'd been offered to purchase a smaller bag, and some other items on the side? My silent hesitation plunged the room into an awkward silence. Nive, apparently misunderstanding my intent…

"Not enough, huh? Well…yeah. I suppose you'd feel that way… I must have caused you to feel some terrible things indeed! Well then, let's do this. A cleaner, more rounded figure. A thousand gold pieces. How's that sound?"

And suddenly there were a hundred more pieces of gold thrown onto the stack. Just how much coin did this adventurer before me have…?

Then again, vampire hunting was quite the lucrative business. Considering that was what Nive did with most of her time, having this much gold wasn't necessarily strange. But then, was it really okay for me to accept such a sum?

I hesitated once more.

I didn't dislike money by any means. In fact, I had quite a fondness for gold and coin. But that wasn't the issue here. Just, to accept that much gold from Nive… It was almost like an invisible string of fate, one I couldn't perceive. Tie us together, and I'd be unable to avoid her in the future…

I'd already taken her little contact scroll. It was far too late to be worrying about anything like that…

But. But then…no. There was that other…

As I continued pondering, wrapped up in my mental debates and troubles, Nive's misunderstanding of the situation simply grew. She threw up her hands, laughing as she did so.

"Mister Rentt! You are really something else when it comes to negotiation, aren't you? Yeah, all right, I get it. I'll double it again. Two thousand gold pieces! No matter how much more you ruminate, Mister Rentt, I don't have any more to give. After all, even I must continue living this life of mine after our little interaction here, you know?"

Saying so, Nive neatly placed 20 platinum pieces on the table.

Platinum…pieces…

S-So many too… The first time I had seen that many… in one place…

I was surprised, stunned, overwhelmed. Deep in my heart and soul.

But I remained outwardly stoic. On this occasion, of all times, I steeled myself. I forbade any external reactions from showing on my features, arming myself with an iron will. Though Nive still didn't seem to understand what I was doing.

"To think you're Bronze-class… Not many people can keep their calm and retain their composure upon seeing this many platinum pieces, you know? Well, maybe if you were a vampire, but you aren't, Mister Rentt. As I thought, you're a suitably rare individual, huh…" Nive said, in a strangely appreciative fashion.

Myullias, who was now next to Nive, was staring at the table herself, her mouth magnificently agape.

Sharl, on the other hand, was simply sighing and shaking his head, the exasperation more than evident in his actions. Perhaps that exasperation was directed at me, the adventurer, who, despite being exposed to the stunning extent of Nive's wealth, merely stood there in relative silence…

"...Still not enough, Mister Rentt?" Nive inquired.

But of course that wasn't the case. Twenty platinum pieces... How could that possibly be insufficient? Any more would be a blatant attempt at fraud. Considering that my life had been endangered, I supposed you couldn't put a monetary value on it, not really. I could go on about this for a while, but it was important to think about things realistically. We adventurers often placed our lives on the line, and more often than not for trivial sums. For me to bring up how priceless a person's life could be, it wouldn't be very convincing, coming from me. Maybe those who had unreasonably risked their lives could say something to that effect. However, when it came to the value of our lives, we, as adventurers, never did give it much stock.

So I replied, trying to illustrate my thoughts, "No, this is enough. There's a magic bag I've been wanting, you see. With this much, I could probably purchase that."

Myullias reacted with surprise. "You do not have a magic bag, yet you transported the carcass of the tarasque all the way into Maalt...?"

Her response revealed that she knew little of the ways of the world. A saint like herself would hardly know of the intricacies of adventurer's guilds.

Nive and Sharl, on the other hand, didn't seem surprised in the slightest. Of course they would know of the magic bag rental services.

Nive turned to her companion. "The adventurer's guild rents out high-capacity magic bags to adventurers for short periods, see? That was what Mister Rentt used to transport the tarasque carcass, Lady Myullias. Not really caught up with worldly stuff, are you?"

Nive turned to me after explaining. I nodded in affirmation.

"There is such a service…? I see. But what would happen if such an item were stolen…?" Myullias started, only to be interrupted unceremoniously by Nive. Short on time perhaps.

"I'll explain all to you later, Lady Myullias, so hold your questions for now, yeah?" Nive said, in a somewhat strict tone of voice.

I could see the defiance on Myullias's features for a second, but she soon nodded, as if convinced.

"But then, Mister Rentt." Nive turned to me once more. "Magic bags are kinda rare, yeah? Even if you really do want one right now, it's not possible to just go and get one, right?"

I nodded calmly. "Yes. But with the funds I have on hand, I can swiftly attend any auction where one is put up for sale. A while ago, a much smaller bag went under the hammer, but I missed that opportunity, and I've regretted it since."

I wasn't even joking—I remembered that day very clearly.

That bag had about half as much spare capacity as my current one, and it had sold for a similar price. I would have been able to afford that, but it was a little too late for such thoughts.

As I pondered the issue, Nive broke the silence with a suggestion.

"Magic pouches and bags are important to an adventurer, yes indeed… Well, then, Mister Rentt! Here's a convenient suggestion for you. Despite your impressions of me and all that, I can be very helpful, see? Just tell me what size bag you're seeking, and I'll spread the word to my contacts. That way, you'll be able to get your bag soon enough, I think."

Hmm… Not a bad suggestion at all. Magic bags and the like were incredibly rare. Well, something like my current bag could be easily arranged for, but one large enough to contain a tarasque…

Even that 1,800-gold bag a while ago was a rarity in and of itself. Given that I was in a town like Maalt, the process would take, say, half a year? No, perhaps even an entire year itself. Magical bags only appeared very rarely in dungeons, so while they could be crafted by craftsmen who specialized in magic items, their numbers were few, and their methods suitably obscured by the various crafting guilds of the land.

Each production run had a limit to it as well, of course. If they were sold at their suggested price, they'd instantly sell out. As such, purchasing these bags through regular channels was all but impossible. All I could do was wait for an existing owner to relinquish their item and offer it up for auction, or retrieve one from the depths of a dungeon. However, the chances of me actually finding one lying around in a dungeon were close to zero. The more normal way of procuring such bags was, unfortunately, none other than the auction.

Taking all that into consideration, and the fact that the exact way to produce these bags remained a secret, known only to a few craftsmen and artisans…

Someone could attempt to copy the product, but up until now no one had actually done it. Or perhaps it was just because the methodology that went into making these bags was top secret. Either way, it was difficult to pinpoint the exact reason.

Though, if I had to guess, the technology by which these bags were created was probably from times of old. Stories told of an ancient kingdom from times long since past, created by a culture and people that were incredibly advanced. Although they'd since ceased to be, the theory was that part of their technologies were passed down. One of these technologies was the magic bag.

Quite the romantic tale.

…There was also the possibility that it was all nothing more than a delusion. No one really knew who had come up with the theory to begin with. And here Nive was saying that all she needed was to spread word and a magic bag would fall into her hands, then into mine. From those words alone, I understood just how useful her network was.

Honestly speaking, I really did want to take her up on her offer. But at the same time, I didn't want anything more to do with Nive.

Perhaps it was because he noticed my reservations, or simply because he saw an opportunity as a merchant, but Sharl leaned in subtly, whispering into my ear.

"If working with Lady Nive is unsettling to you, I can assist you in your search, as well. Our establishment may take a little longer than Lady Nive's network, but we are merchants with many contacts. And if you find that you cannot trust me, Sir Rentt, I would be happy to introduce you to another store. Yes, even the Witta Company."

I hadn't spoken to Sharl about the Witta Company at all. Perhaps he heard about it from his employee.

To the Stheno Company, Witta was a rival, a competitor, a thorn in their side—yet he was willing to introduce me? Was it a means of earning a favor from their competitor? For bringing a deal worth a few thousand pieces of gold to their doorstep?

No. In such a case, it'd be much more advantageous for his own company to conduct the deal. Even so, Sharl was willing to introduce me to another company, in which case, this must have been a sincere gesture on his part.

Thinking about everything that had happened here, I'd been deceived, time and time again, but he must have had unique circumstances of his own as well. Then there was the fact that he was dealing with Nive here, who hardly listened to what anyone else had to say unless it had something to do with vampires... Sharl didn't have much of a choice in the matter, and yet he still offered to do everything he possibly could, even introducing me to a competitor. I felt like he'd already gone above and beyond.

I could leave the task to them then, if it was just procuring a magic bag of the right capacity. If they were unable to do it, then I'd just have to use the platinum pieces I had received in some way or other.

Ah... Coin disappeared much like sea foam—in the blink of an eye. Losing wealth was painful. I'd prefer not to lose any amount of coin to begin with, if possible. I was quite the miser myself. Being broke was certainly better than losing your life—was how I felt about it.

The hushed whispers between Sharl and myself caught the attention of Nive.

"Well, that's fine too, yeah? I'll go look either way. If Mister Sharl here can't get it done even if he tries his darndest, then contacting me is okay too. How about that?"

We'd taken care to be secretive about it, with lowered voices and all that, but there was Nive, casually listening in on everything again. Did she possess an unreasonably acute sense of hearing?

"...I suppose we could, yes."

"Hah. I guess you really hate having anything to do with me, huh? No choice, I suppose. But...just one more thing. One last request."

Ah, yes. Nive's request. She had said something to that effect.

I nervously listened on, wondering what more it was she could possibly want...

"If you find a vampire, do send a report along, yeah? That's what I'd like to say, but you're pretty good yourself, Mister Rentt. You're blessed with divinity, so maybe it'd be faster for you to defeat the monsters yourself. In that case, I'll hold off on that one request of mine," Nive said.

I had assumed she was going to give me a speech about how all vampires were her prey and hers only, but it seemed that wasn't the case.

I grew curious.

"You don't mind? If I slay them instead, I mean."

Nive nodded. "Nope. To me, slaying vampires as I do is a job, but…honestly? It's more of a time-wasting activity. A hobby. Something I do because I'm free, you know? That's a more honest assessment. So it really doesn't matter to me who slays them in the end."

A surprising declaration. So much devotion and dedication for a time-wasting hobby? Even Myullias, saint of the Church of Lobelia, seemed surprised. Sharl was no exception either. I supposed even he hadn't heard of this through his merchant information networks.

This quirk of Nive's could prove to be valuable information. I wasn't quite sure how many individuals she dealt with regularly, but such information could be used by those who didn't want to run into her at all.

"So," Nive continued on, "if you do find any vampires, Mister Rentt, slay them! That's all fine and good, but…"

There it is…

What was it this time? To inform her if I did run across one? I couldn't possibly think of anything else. It didn't seem like she had any more need for coin. Was it power? Influence? No, she already had personal connections and networks that dwarfed even a Platinum-class adventurer's.

Alcohol, then? She certainly seemed like she could drink. Though, she didn't look like the type who drank at all, or even gambled. If she did, she'd likely bankrupt the house.

What was left then…? Women? Nive herself was a woman, so… men? No… It was impossible for me to envision her wanting to be spoiled and pampered by a bevy of men. The individual before me didn't seem to have such needs.

It was no good. I didn't know. I didn't have the slightest inkling.

Thoughts raced through my mind, eventually interrupted by Nive's voice.

"Well, Mister Rentt. If you ever come across a vampire you don't think you could win against, then contact me. That is all I ask of you."

"What do you mean by that, exactly…?"

I couldn't understand Nive's motivations. I understood what she wanted, but why would she want me to do such a thing to begin with? In the end it must all boil down to her merely wanting to slay vampires…

Was she anticipating I wouldn't win and would just let the monster escape? I'd certainly run if I saw no chance of victory, but in such a case, I'd do my due diligence and inform someone who could slay it. That went without saying.

No matter how much I wanted to have absolutely nothing more to do with Nive, this person was undoubtedly skilled in her field of vampire slaying. It made more sense for me to contact her even if I didn't want to. It certainly beat informing the average adventurer. The casualties would simply increase with the latter. Even Nive could read that much into the situation.

Considering this entire series of events, I understood that she hated vampires, enough to orchestrate this grand deception. That was the type of person Nive Maris was. She of all people would be able to read and predict the movements of others. What a certain individual would do when confronted with a certain situation, and other small details like that.

Even the nature of her request was the same. For her to bring it up only after the price of the tarasque parts had been settled... She really was good at her game. My impression of her prior had been mostly negative, and I wouldn't have agreed even if she begged me to do it. If anything, I would've simply ignored her, or refused to cooperate. But now...

She'd already paid me so much in coin. I felt I should at least listen to her simple request. It was just a request, after all. To think it would be so simple...

But behind that request was a huge risk. It was a mere outline of an ominous shadow that I could barely see. It made me want to avoid her at all costs.

Nive, however, was much like a wild beast, in the sense that she didn't seem like the type to let go once she had latched onto something. My interactions with her thus far affirmed this. It didn't matter who it was or what it was about. If Nive Maris wanted to get involved in something, she was going to get involved one way or another.

As such, it finally occurred to me that avoiding her was pointless. In that case, I could just hear her out...

Nive immediately took me up on my offer. "There's not much to it, see. But yeah, you won't believe me even if I say it that way, would you? Allow me to explain then, Mister Rentt."

The way she said it, almost like she'd misunderstood me once again and was giving me more credit than I deserved. But that wasn't the case. Come to think of it, what happened just now was most likely not a misunderstanding either. If anything, I had a feeling Nive had already decided on the final figure from the very beginning and was just increasing it slowly to string me along.

While that in and of itself wasn't a bad thing to me, everything that had happened up until now didn't serve to paint a very favorable image of Nive, I felt.

Yet I was already here. I no longer had much of a choice in the matter…

"Why so tense?" Nive continued. "It's not that important of a topic, yeah?"

Nive smiled. That did little to dispel the almost-visible tension hanging in the air. Myullias, Sharl, and I were all blanketed by a feeling of unease, unsure of what Nive would say next.

I had my mask on, doing my best to suppress my emotions. My body was also still that of an undead, so I didn't sweat much, and didn't subconsciously do so when I was unsettled either.

A quick glance at the other two, however, was enough to perceive the small beads of sweat on their foreheads. We were all about to become privy to a certain secret of Nive Maris, vampire hunter. If you thought about it that way, their reactions made sense.

"You see, I've always been chasing this one specific vampire. All this time."

"Just the one…? Why so?"

An adventurer pursuing a specific vampire wasn't entirely unheard of. If an adventurer's relative, friend, or acquaintance had their blood drained by a vampire, eventually dying and turning into a thrall, then surely said adventurer would be consumed by hate. They'd pursue the beast, seeking revenge. It wasn't unheard of by any means.

This wasn't limited to vampires, of course. It could be a monster, another human being—the result would be the same. It would just be an individual chasing something or someone else in their quest for vengeance.

If there was one thing I could ask… Would they have acted in the same way Nive did? Judging by how she treated others, she didn't seem capable of harboring much hatred. If anything, she hardly cared about those around her, and simply did whatever she pleased. It wouldn't be an exaggeration for me to say she'd hardly care if her friends and family lost their lives.

Perhaps I was being biased, but the way she acted and carried herself strongly suggested such a character and personality. But all this did little to change the reality that Nive was pursuing a certain vampire.

The reason…

"Hmm. What is it, indeed? It's kinda romantic, yeah? Think about it this way, Mister Rentt. Surely you've dreamt of crawling through ancient ruins and dungeons and locating equally ancient objects of power, right? Powerful magic items and the like."

Just like that, the conversation took a strange turn.

I nodded slowly, answering, "Yes, well, I do enjoy old and strange magic items."

Like the little airship. There was no need for me to be that specific though. I really didn't want to provide her with any sort of information at all. If I said anything about liking the little airship, she'd surely follow up with yet another unreasonable request, like getting one for herself as a souvenir. Terrible.

"I'm the same way, yeah?"

"Meaning…?"

"You see, the vampire I'm after, right? It's an old, no, *ancient* existence. It is tremendously feared—the one vampire standing at the very apex of vampires…"

"The twilight vampire, you see."

A smile crept on Nive's lips…

"That's absurd! Twilight vampires don't exist. They are nothing more than a contemporary fairy tale, for the express purposes of scaring children," Lady Myullias, saint of the Church of Lobelia, muttered, shaking her head as she did so.

Nive snorted at her reaction. "Oh, you think that, yeah? Or were you taught that? By the church, I mean. But no, I get it. Oh, I get it. The higher-ups at the church would love it if that were true, no?"

"What are you—"

Myullias had only started half her retort. Before she could finish, however, Nive interrupted her once more.

"Oh, my apologies. It's not like I'm making fun of the church, you know? But Lady Myullias, give it some thought, yeah? I bet my entire life chasing this twilight vampire around, all over the place. You can see as much, right? From everything I've said and done up till now. And yet, you would dismiss its existence as some fairy tale without any sort of evidence or compelling argument? Anyone would get slightly annoyed, yeah?"

Nive's reasoning made perfect sense. What she was saying was indeed correct. Anyone who had their dream made fun of would be sure to lose their temper.

But despite that, I still held my suspicions about Nive. She wasn't really angry at all, was she? She was most likely just saying all this to provoke Myullias. That was how it looked to me.

As for which of these were correct, I had no idea. Maybe they were both correct. It was impossible for me to tell from Nive's demeanor alone. Perhaps that much was to be expected. There was no way she was saying this just so Myullias could understand her point of view.

This woman had a terrible personality...

What did Myullias believe to be true then? Perhaps it was because she realized that Nive's words had some truth to them that she responded with, "Yes. I suppose that is the case. I apologize for my insensitive words."

She apologized somewhat honestly. But she still had more to add.

"I must ask, however, that you refrain from criticizing the teachings and thoughts of the Church of Lobelia any further. The church's teachings are always right."

While it seemed that Nive still had many opinions to state on the matter, she seemingly held her tongue, as if to avoid adding any more tension to the now relatively calmer situation.

Nive instead contended with these vague, ambiguous words. "… Yeah, I guess. Everyone is free to believe in what they want, no?"

Although that seemed like another provocation in and of itself, Myullias didn't seem to mind, or probably just let it slide. She was a little late on the uptake, but it was the wisest choice in this situation, considering we were dealing with Nive.

Immediately after, Nive turned to me. "I'm sure you've heard of twilight vampires, Mister Rentt?"

Oh, but of course. They were featured prominently in fairy tales told to me when I was a child, and in various myths and legends too. I'd also looked into the matter after becoming a vampire myself, hoping to find some sort of hint. As for the fruits of my investigation, I hadn't discovered much, other than some nostalgia about the tales I'd heard in my childhood. Even so, it was a relatively good read.

The twilight vampire was quite a famous villain in children's picture books, plays, performances, and the like. When we used to play-act as heroes and knights back at the village, the weakest, smallest child typically had to play the role of the twilight vampire.

This usually led to them being dogpiled and beaten, so it was a most terrifying role.

While the hero responsible for slaying the twilight vampire varied greatly depending on the location and age of the audience, they were most often some sort of holy knight, or some practitioner of divinity. This image of the hero had endured the test of time because the vampire in question had been framed as an evil existence. Even so, no one really knew who had slain the twilight vampire, or when it had actually happened, so such heroes might well have been the result of wildly speculative storytelling.

In that case, it meant the twilight vampire had been defeated long, long ago. However, there were quite a few holes in that general line of reasoning. If said vampire truly was slain, its corpse, or ashes, would be interred in some grave somewhere in the lands. The fact that Nive continued chasing this being meant she viewed this grave as nothing more than a fake—a red herring of sorts.

"Yes, I've heard of it countless times. We play-acted as heroes and knights as children...although I was always the one who ended up playing the twilight vampire."

"I see... But looking at you now, you really don't look like the type to get bullied when you were younger, yeah?"

Nive had seen through my noncommittal answer almost immediately. I had more to add.

"About that... According to what I heard from a friend at the time, I was seen as quite the odd child. But I've long since mended ties with those who bullied me back then. We get along well enough to talk when I return to my hometown, at least."

"How rare indeed," Sharl piped up with an observation of his own. "Most of the time, if a child who was the victim of bullying returned to their hometown after becoming an adventurer, it would mostly be for revenge. I, for one, would definitely give them a few good knocks. Have you not thought of doing such things, Sir Rentt?"

I thought for a while before giving my answer.

"Well...yes. I suppose. It's been so long, though, so why now? Besides, there are other things I want to do. I hadn't even given the hypothetical situation of me seeking revenge much thought."

"'Other things'...?"

"Yes. To one day become a Mithril-class adventurer."

I'd thought Sharl wouldn't take my statement so seriously. This was the first time I'd spoken of my dream to someone else ever since becoming a vampire. It was a strange feeling.

Of course, I'd said the exact same thing when I was still alive, and quite often at that. But I felt like I was just stubbornly saying it, with no basis whatsoever. Now... Now, I felt a hope in me. As if my wish could, *would* actually come true. I was no longer saying it out of stubbornness or spite. It was now a goal I calmly stated.

Honestly, if I continued growing stronger and stronger at my current pace, then one day...

Of course, no one in this room would understand my circumstances. Not Nive, not Myullias, not Sharl. They were probably laughing at me silently, thinking I was a fool.

That was what had happened when I was still alive. I was laughed at quite often. While fewer people mocked me as time went by, it was hard to take a new adventurer fresh out the gates seriously if they had declared such a thing.

But Nive here...

"Ho... Is that right? In that case, it's a competition to see who gets there first, yeah? I mean, I'm Gold-class now and all, and I'm moving at a good pace, but the goal is far, see."

Myullias offered her observations next. "You are, after all, an adventurer who slew a tarasque all alone. I wouldn't be surprised if that really did come to pass one day."

"If you do ever get there, Sir Rentt," Sharl chimed in, "please support our humble shop. We would be able to charge a premium then!"

He said this, most likely half in jest, as you would normally be invited to use a certain shop's wares upon becoming Mithril-class, be it equipment or tools. This wasn't an altruistic thing to do by any means, seeing as tools a Mithril-class adventurer used often made for good sales. Their patronage, in turn, would bring the shop a great deal of business. The shops would practically be using the Mithril-class adventurer to a certain extent.

There was only one problem: said adventurers were exceedingly rare. In fact, many of these adventurers disliked the social obligations that came with their status and often kept to themselves. Adventurers were made up of many people like that.

As for me, if I ever did become Mithril-class, what would I do? Thinking about it, I preferred to choose my own equipment. The same applied for tools and the like. I wouldn't have much use for a shop offering me free wares then...

Whatever the case, the three people before me didn't scoff at or mock my dream. It was a strange feeling.

Back when I yet lived, at least one of the three would have brushed me off, laughing all the while. Was it because they were good people, then? No, I couldn't really say that. At the very least, they didn't seem like the type to belittle other's beliefs.

"Perhaps, someday. I don't yet know when. Though I would respectfully refrain from any competition or endorsements," I continued on, addressing the three people before me. "More importantly, we should return to the topic at hand, of the twilight vampire. Do you really believe it still lives on, Lady Nive…?"

With that, the conversation was back on its proper railings.

"Oh, I believe it. That's why I'm a vampire hunter now, see?" Nive said, her eyes filled with a myriad of emotions—emotions I couldn't really read.

Was it admiration? Anger? Rage? Duty…? Had she had that look in her eyes when I'd spoken of becoming a Mithril-class adventurer? Or was it something else altogether…?

"Is that so… May I ask why then? Perhaps it'd be rude of me to ask, but from what I understand, the twilight vampire was already slain long ago. That's the common take on it anyway."

"Yes, indeed," Myullias agreed. "It was slain by a priest of the Church of Lobelia, a stake driven through its heart."

Sharl, too, had something to say about the legend. "…Well, the Church of Lobelia may claim that, but other religions and churches also claim it was one of their own who slayed the beast. There are quite a few twilight vampire graves scattered across the lands, as I'm sure you are aware."

The merchant spoke with a vaguely unreadable expression.

While Myullias seemed a little put off by this, Sharl did have a point. For now, the saint held her tongue. There was no way he would openly criticize the Church of Lobelia in front of her, but he could hardly be faulted for a general statement that had some degree of truth in it.

It was as Sharl said, however. I could clearly recall similar information from the tomes I'd read about the matter when it came to the vampire's graves. The most famous grave was the one claimed and advertised by the Church of Lobelia, though. This was, without a doubt, the true grave of the twilight vampire, they would say. However, the truth of it was…

Nive, as if having similar thoughts, soon interjected. "It's as you say, Mister Sharl. Weird, yeah? That there are so many graves here and there. To begin with, there are no clear records of who exactly it was that slayed the twilight vampire. So isn't it natural to assume it hasn't been slain at all?"

Given what had occurred thus far and the evidence at hand, Nive's argument was convincing to a certain degree. But there was still one issue…

"According to the legends, twilight vampires bask in acts of terrible violence. They desire blood, destruction, and the massacre of innocents. If one really existed, here and now, wouldn't it be strange for us to not at least hear of such events?"

They were beings of legend, immensely powerful and capable of swallowing and placing an entire kingdom under its reign. The veracity of such a claim was up in the air, of course, but it was safe to assume twilight vampires usually brought with them a fair amount of destruction. Evil vampires of legend often brought about disasters and such simply by existing.

But there were no records for the past few centuries of any vampire-related incidents, or anything resembling such. If this twilight vampire really were alive, then disasters were sure to have happened, right? That was the greatest evidence disproving the existence of the twilight vampire thus far.

"Well, they aren't mindless beasts, you know? It's normal to assume they could've very well faked their own death and went into hiding. When it comes to vampires, lesser vampires aside, greater vampires don't really need that much blood if they are only seeking to maintain their existence, see? If a vampire wants to live quietly, unseen, then a greater vampire would do much better in that regard. Consider, then, how a twilight vampire would fare…"

That was something I didn't know. Greater vampires weren't observed often, so much of their ecology and habits remained a mystery. Nive, on the other hand, would know much more about this, seeing how she was a vampire hunter in the first place.

But then… Hmm. So a greater vampire doesn't require as much blood to survive…?

I personally only needed three drops or so a day. Was that a great amount? Or was it not very much at all? If I had to say, I'd be on the lesser side of the scale, right?

Curious, I posed a question to Nive.

"Since we're on the topic, how much blood does a lesser vampire usually require?"

"Hmm… Depends on the individual, see? I can't give you exact numbers, but say an estimate of, uh, two whole humans per month? Somewhere around there, yeah? For an estimate…around ten full fills of that flower vase over there, I think," Nive said, pointing to an ornamental vase on display. "A middle vampire would need about half that, and a greater vampire, probably half of the previous. Something along those lines. If they went any higher than that, then they'd need even less… It's hard to describe these things in words, yeah?"

The vase wasn't terribly large; it would fill five cups or so at most. And…ten vases worth of blood was needed? That was a terrifyingly huge amount.

No… Maybe I simply required too little? Was I a greater vampire then? The thought crossed my mind, but it was most likely just me overthinking things. After all, Nive did mention that appetites varied by the individual. I had a strong hunch my lessened appetite was more of a quirk.

Would there ever be a day where I could be sure of what exactly I was…? A difficult task, to say the least. Whatever the case, I should return to the conversation at hand.

"I see. I understand. Well, then, was your request for me to contact you should I ever discover a twilight vampire, Lady Nive? Nothing else?"

A final verification of her request. Was this all she wanted, in the end?

Nive nodded, then…

"Yeah, that's fine. But Mister Rentt. You won't be able to tell just by looking at them, right?"

"That… Yes, it's as you say. What do twilight vampires even look like?"

If I didn't know even that, then there was no way I could search for anything.

Nive shook her head, speaking without a second of hesitation or doubt. "I have absolutely no idea."

…*Are you joking, lady? You don't know, yet you ask this of me…?* That was what I wanted to say. But I couldn't raise my protests in the face of Nive's serious expression.

"Yes, yes," she continued on. "I know it's kinda ridiculous for me to ask something like that of you. That was why I said that just now, yeah? That if you ever meet a vampire you can't win against, Mister Rentt, you contact me."

So that was all this was about...?

"So you mean to say, Lady Nive, that I cannot win against a twilight vampire?"

Of course the conversation would head in that direction. At least, Nive clearly didn't think I was capable.

But...she was right. I wouldn't be able to win. It was impossible. Even I knew that. I just thought I should ask...

Nive quickly offered a response. "Didn't mean to snub you, yeah? I can apologize for that... But see, a twilight vampire is a monster that destroys entire kingdoms and whatnot. If you could do the same, Mister Rentt, then I'd have no complaints whatsoever..."

Of course I can't do that! ...And that was what Nive implied.

I could do no such thing. Not me. If I could, I'd already be a Mithril-class adventurer.

But did this mean Nive was capable of such a thing? That was a little too terrifying to imagine...

Even so, adventurers were quite perceptive to the strengths of others around them, and also often interested in such.

So I asked, "And you claim to be able to do this yourself, Lady Nive?"

A fair amount of laughter accompanied her response.

"Hah! Of course not! I'm just saying I can put up quite the fight if the opponent is a vampire, see? Even if the enemy was insanely strong, there would at least be a chance of victory for me. In other words, bridge the gap with skills and know-how, technique, and experience, and you get someone like me."

Her response was more realistic and grounded than I thought it would be.

I see. So this was why I wouldn't be able to do it—I lacked all those things. I was wholly convinced. Well, there was that, and also the fact that Nive was much stronger than me to begin with... In any case, I now had a better understanding of the situation, and I nodded at her to signal as such.

"I understand. In that case, if I ever come across a vampire like that, I will be sure to contact you."

Saying so, I extended my hand. A handshake, for appearances. Maybe it was a bit of a friendly gesture, or just something to settle our differences, given everything that had transpired.

Nive's eyes seemed to widen ever so slightly upon seeing my hand.

"...Yeah. Hope we can work together from here on out," she replied, grasping my hand. The smile on her face was a little softer. It was a smile I hadn't seen up until now.

Epilogue

"Oh, you're back, I see. How was it then?"

Lorraine's voice was the first thing I heard as I opened the doors to her abode, finally having returned from the Stheno Company.

Lorraine's voice... I was finally back home. Such was the emotion that welled up from the bottom of my heart.

I'd crossed a rather precarious bridge this time; even I understood that. Perhaps I'd been a little careless, but it was simply not possible to imagine such a chain of events. I was only heading off to sell some materials. It was as rare as a meteor falling on my head as I walked the open streets of Maalt.

Even if nothing happened to me this time, that woman, Nive, had quite the intuition when it came to sniffing out vampires. We would surely cross paths again someday.

"Quite a few...unexpected things happened. But I'm fine."

"What...? Have you gotten yourself embroiled in some strange affair again?" Lorraine said, an expression of mild irritation on her face. She did, however, seem willing to listen to what I had to say.

"In any case, come sit down, and speak your mind."

Lorraine sighed as I finished explaining most of the situation. "...Nive Maris, and a saint of the Church of Lobelia...

Easily individuals you would not want to cross paths with, Rentt, no matter how you think about it."

I nodded in response. "Honestly. It's as you say… But Nive has a special technique to detect vampires, or so she claims. It had no effect on me whatsoever. Perhaps I could say I was lucky this time."

"Ah, yes. That Holy Fire you mentioned, right? I've seen a practitioner of it, back in my hometown. At the time, it was seen as a very rare technique, zealously guarded by the churches. As such, the details were hazy to say the least, but it was quite interesting when I set about investigating it. Alas, no one would tell me a thing, even if I inquired. To begin with, it is said that those who do not have any blessings of divinity are unable to see it, yes? That would mean the practitioner back at my hometown made it so their flames would be visible… Hmm. I'd requested to see it so I could understand the underlying mechanics of it better, but they would not cooperate, you see.

"On another note… That detection technique had no effect on you? Even if you are indeed some sort of vampire?"

Even I couldn't really answer that question. Nive confidently claimed she was able to detect and discover vampires without fail. If I were to accept that truth for what it was, and expand on that train of thought…

"…Maybe I'm not a vampire at all…?" I muttered, more to myself than to anyone else. Lorraine pondered this for a while, too, before offering her opinion.

"Not impossible, I would say. To begin with, there is no way for us to affirm that you really are a vampire. Skeleton, ghoul, thrall, vampire… Visually, you have been evolving from one undead monster to the next, yes? All we did was assume that you may be some sort of vampire. You weren't very much of a standard skeleton even back when you were a pile of walking bones. Taking all that into consideration, it is hardly impossible."

Lorraine did have a point, albeit a pointed, difficult one.

As she said, I didn't know very much about my existence as I was right now, and that was how I'd honestly put it. Was I a monster? Was I not? The lines were vague and ambiguous at best. I really had no idea.

But based on what we'd observed thus far, the likelihood of me being a monster was indeed high. If anything, I was a monster of some kind, if the current line of reasoning was to be believed.

If I were to turn that around and consider what Lorraine said, though, had I simply been a skeleton-like being, but not actually a skeleton, since the very beginning? At that rate, no explanations would prove satisfactory. In that case, my predictions for the future would hinge on the progress I'd made up until this point.

Regardless, I'd been evolving this entire time, much like the Existential Evolution of monsters. That much was fine—it would be a reference of sorts, if nothing else.

Lorraine had spent far more time pondering that topic as opposed to me.

"It may be a little late for this particular commentary, Rentt, but we already knew from the beginning that you were different than the average monster. You mentioned it just now, no? That divinity has no effect on you. That would be because you are special, Rentt. That is the obvious conclusion. Knowing that much may just be enough at this point. The next most obvious possibility would be the fact that you were blessed with reserves of divinity, unlike the typical undead. Could that not be the cause?"

"Divinity, huh…"

According to Nive, vampires were weak to divinity. There was simply no way a vampire that utilized divine powers existed.

I, however, was able to wield my divinity just fine. As to why I was still able to use it even after becoming a vampire-like creature, I had no idea. Perhaps it was a trait carried over from life?

At the very least, the sensations and feelings I experienced while using divinity hadn't changed one bit. Of that I could be sure. Was Lorraine suggesting that merely possessing divinity within oneself made one impervious to it, even if it was used on me by others?

Holy Fire supposedly caused great pain to vampires, if Nive's words were to be believed. I hardly felt that way about divinity at all. Was that why it didn't work…? Because I was some special vampire-like existence, but not quite a vampire at all? That did seem easier to believe…

Lorraine continued. "It's the same way for poisons, magic, and the like. If an individual has a resistance of some kind, said attacks would be ineffective or nullified. That much is to be understood. Simple, yes? Rentt, from what I recall, your divinity came from you repairing an old shrine back in your hometown?"

I'd described to Lorraine a while ago why I was blessed with divinity in the first place. It wasn't a big deal, so I had no reason to hide it.

Among the friends I had in life, few individuals knew I was blessed with all three powers. It was incredibly rare, but I was unable to develop my potential. Or perhaps I was simply a jack-of-all-trades. Such was the case in the past.

It was, by all means, quite the accurate description…

"Yes. It was quite run-down… In fact, it had been mostly swallowed up by the trees in the forest. Its existence wasn't even known to the greater half of the villagers in my hometown. It was a bit of a pity, I thought… So I got rid of the shrubbery around it, cleaned it up, and mended whatever parts that were broken.

It took me a while, but this was before I became an adventurer. I had a great amount of free time."

"You say it so simply, Rentt. That you fixed a shrine and that was that. Quite some skill was required for that despite what you say, no?"

"A carpenter from the village taught me what I needed to know. I had an eye for detail and precision. I learned the basics relatively quickly, and the rest was just trial and error. It was good training, to say the least."

"Capable as ever, I see... Even so, you lacked the capacity to progress as an adventurer, of all things. The gods are cruel, no?"

"I wouldn't really say so, no. After all, I'm now more than capable of aiming for the top. Perhaps the gods were actually relatively merciful in my case."

"You are far too positive, Rentt. But alas, that is indeed one of your good traits. But you said it was a shrine, yes? What god was it built in dedication to?"

"Well..." I didn't really have a concrete answer. "I don't know. It was a shrine no one visited, after all. Perhaps the village elders would know something about it..."

"Is that right... Well, then, Rentt. Should we make a trip to this village of yours?" Lorraine said, suddenly and without warning.

"Make a trip, you say…? But why, Lorraine?"

Lorraine's answer was swift. "To understand you better. Everything that can be investigated should be investigated. That's how I feel about it. Your divinity is especially important with regards to this. It is a crucial element when it comes to understanding what you currently are. At the very least, should we not investigate the gods or spirits that bestowed their blessing upon you?"

As usual, Lorraine had a point. However, the possibility of anyone in the village knowing of the shrine was slim. If they did, would they not have sought to repair it themselves? That seemed obvious to me.

"It may be a fruitless trip."

"Then so be it, if that is indeed the case. But you yourself said it, Rentt, did you not? That the elder may know something about this shrine of yours, yes?"

I did indeed say that, yes…but the possibility was slight. It wasn't something I'd said out of certainty. Even so, we could just ask.

"I suppose, yes."

"There is a possibility, right?" Lorraine continued pressing her point. "Then there would be some worth in going. Do you not think so?"

"Even then, it's by no means close to where we are, Lorraine. A return trip would take us about two weeks, in terms of distance…"

My hometown was a rural village. Maalt was a rural township on the border of the Kingdom of Yaaran, but my village, Hathara, was even more rural than that. It was so far that I'd only returned a few times ever since coming to Maalt.

My income before had been precarious. I simply didn't have enough coin to stop adventuring for two weeks and pay my hometown a visit. I did try to save, with the aim of returning once every year, but…

"You say that, Rentt, but surely it's not as removed from civilization as the Great Forest of Ramuze? Or the Floating Ruins of Hohel?"

Lorraine's questions were exasperating. I sighed, responding in an adequately annoyed fashion.

"Of all the things to say, Lorraine. Such comparisons are a little too extreme. It's a rural village, but traveling merchants do visit from time to time. We have roads, you know."

The two examples Lorraine raised were places of mystery. People couldn't get to them even if they wished to do so, and they really shouldn't be going there in the first place. So severe were the restrictions that licenses and permits were required to enter, depending on the season and range of exploration.

My hometown, Hathara, was nothing like that. At the very least, anyone could enter freely. It was a response made in frustration. But Lorraine…

"See? Then it's fine, is it not? In addition, you have not returned for several years now. It is a good time. There are no longer any financial restrictions either. At the very least, you would not have to limit your expenses terribly and live off wild flora that you find naturally growing around these parts, like you did in the past."

When she put it that way…

For some reason, I felt like this had all gone according to Lorraine's plan. No…it wasn't just a feeling. Lorraine had most likely wanted to lead me to this point from the start.

The way we thought was simply too different. Perhaps I never really had a say in the direction of the conversation to begin with.

"Well...I guess so..."

"And there is the fact that Nive Maris is currently in Maalt. Some distance between you and her is not exactly a bad thing."

That was a point I could readily agree on. Nive was most likely here in search of a vampire that wasn't me, and she'd most likely continue her search. That, in turn, may cause my identity to be revealed.

I'd been bathed in Holy Fire and wasn't worse for wear, hence I wasn't a vampire. That much was fine, but Nive didn't seem like the type to completely let her guard down just because of that. So long as I stayed in this town, I'd surely cross paths with her at some point.

With that in mind, I could easily use this chance to leave Maalt and eventually return when things were a little calmer. While it might seem suspicious of me to leave town after being questioned by Nive, all I had to do was inform someone of the date of my return. There'd be little incentive for Nive to simply leave Maalt behind to chase after me, especially if she still thought there may be a vampire lurking in the town.

But there was still one problem.

"It's not a bad suggestion, Lorraine. But I do have an ongoing request. Unless my client agrees with what I have to say, this trip will be impossible."

The ongoing request in question came from none other than Laura, in which I had to regularly pick Dragon Blood Blossoms.

Lorraine seemed to have already anticipated this... "Yes, I am aware. You would have to discuss this with your client, Rentt. If it really is impossible, I will set out on this trip alone. There is one more thing I—well, you, too, Rentt—would have to put on hold:

Alize's training. We would have to inform her that she would be taking a short break."

Ah, there was that, as well.

Alize's training periods were irregular. She had quite a few duties at the orphanage, after all, and she only attended sessions when her schedule permitted it. Plus, the goal wasn't to have Alize become an adventurer right away. Lorraine and I thought in the long term. When Alize came of age to register as an adventurer, she'd already have some degree of knowledge and capability. She had the time to train slowly, so a break or two wouldn't be too bad.

"There are some other matters here and there, nothing difficult to settle by any means. More importantly, Rentt, who exactly would you be going as?"

Lorraine was most likely asking if I would be going as Rentt Vivie or Rentt Faina. That was a troublesome question. However, considering I had to speak at length with the elders and reveal the fact that I was the one who'd repaired that shrine, I had no choice but to go as myself in this particular case.

There was the ever-present worry that I might inadvertently cause my false identity to unravel, but at this point, I no longer cared if my false identity was uncovered. I now looked the same as I had in life. I wore a mask, but a single look at the top or bottom half of my face would surely allow them to remember.

As for me registering twice at the guild... If the guild really wanted to nitpick, yes, it would be a violation of the rules. Even so, the punishment, if any, would most likely not be severe. The most severe punishment doled out by the guild would be removing an adventurer's name from its ranks, in addition to a worldwide ban at all the guilds across the lands. Such punishments were only delivered when an adventurer caused great harm to the guild, committed genocide or other serious crimes, or had plotted against their kingdom or country. Punishment for registering twice would be light by comparison. In the worst-case scenario, it would be a fine of a few gold coins.

Thinking about it, there were quite a few people who registered twice. If anything, the guild may simply overlook my transgressions. Most adventurers were people with a checkered past, with certain individuals unable to reveal any details about their previous lives. Some individuals simply didn't want to operate under the name they'd used before. Taking all these factors into consideration, registering twice wasn't a rare occurrence.

The guild, of course, knew about all this; it just chose to keep quiet about it in most cases. As a result, I could hardly imagine that I would be dealt with harshly.

I would cross that bridge when I came to it, but even then there would surely be avenues for negotiation. The guild was neither a strictly good nor bad organization, so it should be fine.

Shelving my thoughts, I looked straight at Lorraine before finally answering her question.

"I will go as Rentt Faina. I could simply change my equipment and change the look of my mask. It should work out...I think."

"Ah, Mister Rentt! What brings you here today?"

The person who called out to me was none other than the Latuule family's gate guard. His name was... Ah. I'd never asked. It seemed Laura or Isaac had informed him of my name in my stead.

"I have certain matters to discuss in regards to a request. Could you please ask for Isaac?"

"Of course... Hmm? Mister Rentt... You seem to be speaking much smoother today," the man said, nodding as he manipulated some sort of magic item he'd withdrawn from his pocket.

I nodded in response. "Yes. I was injured before and couldn't speak properly. But I've since recovered, as you can hear."

The man seemed convinced. "Haha, know a good healer or two, Mister Rentt? Whatever the case, that's good to hear. Master Isaac will be here soon. Please wait for a little while."

The man looked at the magic item in his hands, then back up at me.

Soon enough, the living hedges of the Latuule family's magical maze reshaped and parted, revealing Isaac coming our way.

It was always a strange sight—plants that had been still just before rustling here and there, rearranging themselves until a door-like passageway was formed. The spectacle before me almost made me feel like shrub ents weren't all that mysterious. Maybe that wasn't a fair comparison, since ents were monsters. Monsters were somewhat removed from the normal ecology of flora and fauna to begin with. It really did seem pointless to think too much about them at times.

Despite this, it was true that monsters obeyed certain basic tenets and laws that governed their existence. That was precisely what scholars like Lorraine investigated. The fruits of their labor greatly benefited adventurers such as ourselves. You should really be grateful to these scholars and their research.

"Well met, Mister Rentt. I see you are not here to deliver Dragon Blood Blossoms today. Are you perhaps here to address another matter...?"

Isaac looked the same as ever with his silver hair and pale skin.

"Yes," I answered his query. "In truth, recent events require me to undertake a journey of sorts. There is the matter of our agreement that I'd like to discuss, if possible..."

"I see. Perhaps it would be best to speak with my master directly then. Please. This way."

With that, Isaac began walking. I would surely become lost in this garden if I lost sight of him, so I quickly followed after.

"Mister Rentt, did you have something to discuss?" Laura asked after we exchanged the relevant pleasantries.

I was now in the guest parlor of the Latuule manor, having been led here by Isaac earlier. Laura's dress today was different than the one she'd worn before. It was pure-white, for starters. The amount of fanciful frills on her being remained the same, though. Did Laura have multiple dresses like this one...? I felt the wealth of the Latuule family just by gazing at the garment.

"Yes. It has come to be that I must make a journey of sorts. It is, however, somewhat far away. If I had to place an estimate on the period of my absence, it would be about two weeks."

"I see. So you wish to terminate the request then? In that case, we could simply suspend it instead. There will be no problems on our end once you continue doing as you have done after returning to Maalt."

Laura's response was unexpected, to say the least. It was a scenario I'd thought of, but more often than not, a terminated request would lead to the client simply searching for another adventurer to take the previous one's place. But Laura did no such thing and was instead suggesting that I resume my duties once I returned to Maalt. It was something to be appreciative of.

Perhaps Laura had picked up on my feelings on the matter, because she said, "Of course, I do trust you, Mister Rentt. Adventurers willing to go to the Tarasque Swamp once every week are relatively rare. In addition, even fewer of such adventurers capable enough to do so know how to properly harvest Dragon Blood Blossoms. As such, I don't have much of a choice other than to rely on you, Mister Rentt."

She did have a point. It was under these circumstances that I was hired to deal with this request in the first place. But Laura could probably find a Gold-class adventurer somewhere for her needs. The fact she didn't do this, and instead selected me for the venture, was indeed something to be grateful for.

"I appreciate your kind understanding. I will immediately contact you upon my return. On another note, perhaps I am simply being nosy, but what will you do in my absence…?"

"I will leave it to Isaac, just like I had before. As such, it would be highly appreciated if you could return at your earliest convenience… Of course, you do not have to expedite your journey on my account. Come to think of it, where are you traveling to? Hmm… No. If you would not like to mention it, I have no intentions of forcing you to tell me," Laura said, suddenly aware of my undisclosed destination.

"I am headed to Hathara village."

A village in the middle of nowhere—a rural village. I assumed Laura wouldn't even know of its existence, but her appearance belied her wisdom and knowledge.

She immediately nodded.

"I see you are going quite far away indeed. Why are you visiting, if I may ask?"

I hesitated at her question. Should I answer her honestly? If I did answer, just how much should I reveal? It was a difficult decision.

Laura would immediately see through a shoddy, half-baked lie. That wouldn't be good for the relationship of trust built between client and adventurer.

With those thoughts in mind, I decided not to reveal the entire truth, but instead give her a limited, but reasonably truthful explanation.

"To tell the truth, there is a small shrine in that village. I am traveling with the intent of visiting it."

"Shrine…? Why though?"

"I have been blessed with great reserves of divinity, you see. That blessing was granted to me by whatever gods or spirits that inhabit the shrine. As to what sort of gods or spirits they may be…I'm not certain. That is why I am traveling there, to discover the identity of my divine patron, so to speak."

Laura nodded plainly at this, without the slightest hint of surprise. I'd told Isaac I possessed divinity when I first crossed paths with him in the swamp, so it wouldn't be strange that Laura, being his employer and master, would know of this as well.

"Divinity… I see. A somewhat rare talent you have, especially since you are an adventurer. But… Hmm. I see… So that is what this is about. I understand. It is said that the blessing of gods and spirits intensifies in power once the blessed individual becomes aware of the identity of their patron."

This was the first time I'd ever heard of that.

"Is that true? I am but a mere amateur when it comes to the applications of divinity. I don't know much at all when it comes to the more intricate details."

"Most individuals gain an understanding of the basic applications of divinity the moment they are blessed. Of those who are blessed with divinity, over half would stop at this point of mastery. It is, however, one of the three great powers, alongside mana and spirit. As such, the proper use of divinity does have quite the long history behind it, along with many techniques to utilize it, most of which are kept secret by the numerous churches and religious bodies across the land."

That did seem true. I had no idea how to reproduce the Holy Fire I'd recently observed. Even if you didn't go to such extreme applications, divinity probably had many other uses beyond strengthening your equipment, body, or basic healing and cleansing.

But there were no avenues of learning when it came to divinity. It'd be absurd for me to go knocking on some religious organization's doors as I was now and undergo training to become some sort of priest. I wanted to become a Mithril-class adventurer, not the priest of fertilizers.

Laura continued, having even more good news for me.

"If you are going to investigate the origins of your divinity, Mister Rentt, why not take some tomes from the Latuule family's collection? Tomes on divinity, of course. Recorded within are several techniques and methodologies for mastering certain applications of divinity, collected from a few churches here and there."

…And just how had she come into possession of such tomes to begin with? Were they not zealously guarded secrets by churches and the like? Inquisitors would surely come knocking if such a thing was brought to light.

But I couldn't deny that it'd be unmistakably helpful in a variety of ways. Not to mention that if I refused on the grounds of fearing a hypothetical inquisition, Lorraine would surely lose her temper at the wasted opportunity.

"Why did you not simply accept it?" she would ask.

So I said, "If I may borrow them, that would be a great help indeed…"

Laura smiled at my response, nodding. "Oh, but of course."

Side Story: The Saint of Healing

My name is Myullias Raiza, and I am a saint of the Church of Lobelia.

When I was young, I received a blessing of divinity from the Goddess Lobelia herself. Once my divinity manifested and began budding, I was whisked away to the church and underwent saint training on a daily basis.

Today was no different.

We came from the Holy Empire of Ars, far, far away. We were here to shine the grace and light of the church on these rural borderlands. With my powers, I could heal a great deal of people and show them the righteousness of the church. Such was why I was here, in the township of Maalt.

…At least, that was how it was supposed to be.

The only chapel of Lobelia present in Maalt was small, to say the least. It was tiny. It was nothing compared to the grand cathedrals in the holy capital of the Holy Empire of Ars. In the holy capital, the cathedrals were massive, like castles and forts. You could say the building in the middle was no castle, but more like a gigantic cathedral.

This Maalt place, however…

Well, I didn't mind small, not really. What surprised me was the behavior of the locals. Not one of them even glanced at the small chapel here. That concerned me somewhat.

Some people did visit the chapel occasionally, but they weren't there for prayers or sermons. Instead, they only wished to purchase the high-quality holy water made by the church, or the soap that had been made from said water. They were just there to purchase.

Well, yes, they did walk up and offer some tithes, contributions, and the like, then offer a prayer or two. No matter how I looked at it, however, they merely *seemed* like they were praying. Their hearts weren't in it; I could see that much.

"What would the Great Church-Father say if he saw all this…?"

Even if I were to overlook the blatant sale of the church's "products," this place was nothing more than a shop, no matter how I viewed it. As soon as I muttered that, a sharp-eyed man who had been standing next to me immediately had something to say.

"The Great Church-Father knows. This is just how it is in rural towns."

"Then…"

Why would he just let it sit? That's what I wanted to say.

But the man, Gilly was his name, shook his head.

"No. It is exactly because the Great Church-Father himself feels sorrow over this situation that he dispatched you here, Lady Myullias. Your responsibility is a heavy one to bear indeed," he said with a serious face while spouting his words.

Was that really true? I was indeed a saint, but I didn't have much experience at all. I'd healed and cleansed some towns before, sure, even given a sermon once or twice… But there were many more priests and saints who were more experienced, more talented, or more filled with divinity than me.

Maybe it was because this was a small border town. Maybe they thought I could do the same thing even if they didn't send out any of their more accomplished members. But even though Maalt was a rural border town, it was quite the large place.

My burdens seemed to grow heavier the more I pondered them. This was why I decided to just speak my mind.

"If the goal were to truly increase the influence of the church, then I wouldn't have been sent. It would have been Sir Aaruz, or Lady Millia."

Both of those individuals were skilled and possessed large reserves of divinity. Even a hundred copies of myself couldn't hope to catch up to them. They were truly the most prominent priest and saint of our generation.

If the church really did want to expand its influence at the border, then someone of their level should have been dispatched instead. Even though I was a saint myself, my ranking was somewhat low. I was on the fringes of the church's ranks, at best. Sending someone like me here had the effect of, say, a single drop of water in an ocean.

I had no idea if Gilly understood what was going through my mind.

"Those two are always the most occupied individuals in the Church of Lobelia. It's difficult to tell which one is busier. With that said, surely you can see it would be all but impossible to send them to faraway lands such as this," he replied, with yet another obvious answer.

I knew that. Those two were much busier than the average noble or royal. It was incomparable. It was said they lived every day by the minute, without any breaks or much time to rest. Of course it'd be impossible for them to come to a faraway place like this.

"So, you mean to say I was sent because I had more free time."

"But of course not, Lady Myullias. It's nothing like that at all…"

He droned on. I thought about listening but quickly changed my mind. I probably wouldn't have been pleased with whatever I heard anyway.

Not to mention, even if I had been sent here simply because I was otherwise unoccupied, it didn't change what I had set out to do. My job was to demonstrate to the people living here the righteous grace of the Church of Lobelia.

Well, I'd do my best, I guessed.

I decided to be more optimistic about it, taking whatever might come…

"The sermon has been scheduled for a week from now, right?" I asked.

"Yes." Gilly was always fast with his responses. "There will be quite some preparations to make until then. We must greet the appropriate influencers and individuals of power in this town as well. Some relatives of these individuals have injuries and illnesses that cannot be cured by conventional healing magics, you see."

I already knew what we had to do then. In exchange for tithes, contributions, and donations, I would heal them, and they would gladly pay their fair share. After all, they were considerably wealthy, and healing of that nature couldn't simply be bought off the street.

With that, the believers in the Church of Lobelia would slowly increase.

In truth, few of this kingdom's common folk believed in the church. The church's influence, however, had spread among noble and merchant families—families with power and resources. These relations, in turn, were formed and reinforced by such activities.

When it came to the common folk, however, blessings weren't given unless they had contributed a fair amount of donations. Needless to say, this didn't help much when it came to increasing the amount of followers in the region.

To make things worse, the dominant religion in this kingdom, the Church of the Eastern Sky, didn't ask for any tithes, nor did they discriminate among social classes. They simply lent their power to all they could reach. As a result, there were cases where the needs of noble and wealthy families weren't prioritized. The Church of Lobelia, prioritizing the rich over the poor, saw an increase in followers among these social castes.

As for which of the churches was correct... If one were to go by their heart, the Church of the Eastern Sky was a clear winner. However, if I were to think about it realistically, it was hard to say.

Suppose a member of one's family fell gravely ill and urgently needed treatment. Because it took a while for them to be checked, they lost their life. No one would want to be in such a situation, which was why they would pay to be healed first. When it came to the Church of the Eastern Sky, the more severely ill were treated before the mildly ill, but some would be inadvertently left behind as a result. The Church of Lobelia focused its efforts on individuals who were left out and would intervene, slowly increasing its sphere of influence. That was how it worked, anyway.

If one were to look at the big picture, it could be said that both churches had their niches and coexisted relatively well, to some degree. The Church of Lobelia wouldn't be satisfied with this alone, of course.

Then there was the consideration that it was an individual's freedom to believe, or not, in a certain religion. From that angle, this kingdom was quite the ideal place.

Now I had to do something about this situation. It was a complicated thing to think about.

As I continued thinking, Gilly began reading a missive that had arrived from the church, turning to me.

"And then...hmm. This is..." He tilted his head slightly to one side.

"What is it...?"

"A direct order from the Great Church-Father himself, you see. But you are instructed to accompany...Gold-class adventurer, Nive Maris? What does this mean...?" he muttered, a troubled expression creeping onto his features.

Who was this Nive Maris, Gold-class adventurer, in the first place? That was my first thought on the matter.

During my time as a saint, I always gathered the knowledge, skills, and techniques required of me. Information and knowledge on adventurers, much less following them around, was hardly part of my curriculum. Of course, depending on the situation, the church received such requests from kings, important nobles, and the like, so even I would know of them if they were a famous Mithril-class adventurer.

But...the name of a mere Gold-class adventurer?

I knew of certain quirky individuals who had their fair share of achievements, or adventurers who might soon make it into the rank of Mithril-class. While these individuals often had many pairs of eyes scrutinizing them, there was no news that I particularly had to pay attention to.

Gilly, however, didn't seem to share my opinion.

"Gold-class adventurer Nive Maris is a famous vampire hunter. As the title suggests, she specializes in hunting vampires."

"A vampire hunter?"

"Yes. More often than not, adventurers choose whatever prey or request that suits their fancy at the time. However, there are occasionally adventurers who, in the name of efficiency or personal preference, hunt a specific monster. This is especially the case when it comes to vampire hunting. They are a difficult monster to hunt, but the returns are proportionally large. While there is no meaning to capturing a mere thrall, capturing the 'lord' of a flock would easily reap quite the fortune. A thousand gold pieces? Perhaps more? It is a…romantic profession to say the least."

Gilly was seemingly worked up for some reason. How rare. If anything, this was quite odd. He normally never had much in the way of emotions in his attitudes and mannerisms.

"You seem to be having fun. Did you wish to become an adventurer at some point?"

"Ah. Please excuse me. Before I became a member of the cloth, there was indeed a time when I was little when I thought of such. I was simply reminiscing."

This man had a somewhat unexpected past. Simply looking at his face made me assume he'd been cold and rigid even as a child, with only a one-track mind and path.

Dreams, hmm… Having put it that way, I supposed I could see it to a certain extent. Of course, even this man before me must have had a time when he was a cute and lovable child. For a child like that to have such thoughts was hardly strange.

For some reason, I'd thought Gilly had been the same as a child as he was now.

"I see... So even someone like you had a relatively normal childhood," I said in an obviously provocative manner. Gilly paid my words no heed.

"But of course. Even I wasn't simply born this way from the start," he replied, as if seeing through my intent from the very beginning. "In any case. About these orders... Saint Myullias Raiza is to accompany Nive Maris, whereupon she will enter a series of negotiations with a certain adventurer. That's what the missive says."

"Negotiations with an adventurer? Why me...?"

I didn't dislike it by any means, but it was mysterious. I did have similar experiences; it was very common for nobles to summon priests and saints to their fancy negotiations, out of fear of poison in their drink for example. With a priest or saint on hand, poisons could be easily cleansed, and I'd been to a few of these events myself.

It seemed my task this time was something similar. Though it wasn't exactly easy to summon a saint of the Church of Lobelia. At the very least, the individual would require privilege, power, and coin. Even a Gold-class adventurer wouldn't be capable of such a thing...or so I thought.

Gilly, as if reading my mind, continued on.

"I don't know. However, this is a direct order from the Great Church-Father himself. It would be safe to assume that Nive Maris is able to influence the upper echelons of the church in some way or another. If not, such an order would be all but impossible."

"Is she really that famous? How would a mere Gold-class adventurer have such powers...?"

This was something not even highly ranked nobles were capable of doing.

While the Church of Lobelia didn't have much influence in the Kingdom of Yaaran, one would be hard-pressed to find a bigger, more established and powerful religious body if they were to scour the lands of the world.

It went without saying that the church had a large degree of influence on the nobles and ruling governments of various countries and kingdoms. To be able to make a direct request of the Great Church-Father himself, the one individual who was the highest authority and power in the Church of Lobelia...

Even Gilly seemed perplexed. "I don't know what to make of that. However, Lady Myullias, I'm afraid it's not within your rights to refuse."

I knew that. I knew that much, but...

"Nive Maris will arrive at this chapel tomorrow," he continued. "You would do well to ask her for the specifics and details then."

I felt a foreboding sense of unease, but I couldn't go against a direct order. All I could do was nod and allow my mind to drift to thoughts of tomorrow...

"Well, hello there, saint Myullias Raiza. I'm Nive Maris. Just your average, boring, Gold-class adventurer. Pleased to make your acquaintance."

The person spoke as they entered the room I was waiting in. She was nothing like any of the individuals I'd dealt with up until this point. I didn't know what to do with her.

Her aura was very similar to that of Sir Aaruz's.

What was different was that twinkle in her eyes. It was almost like she was licking her lips in anticipation of the hunt, as if she were standing before her prey. Such was the unease I felt as I stood before this person.

"Yes. The pleasure is all mine. If I may ask…I've been summoned to accompany you to a negotiation with a certain adventurer…?"

I wanted to be rid of her as soon as possible, getting right to the topic at hand.

"Ah, yeah. Lady Myullias, you're a practitioner of cleansing divinity, right? I'm not all that great with that, see. They can be pretty cunning and all that. I don't think I've been found out. But we have to be careful if any food or drink is spiked, you know? Can't be too careful."

I couldn't understand a single word. I tilted my head in confusion.

"They…? Who is this 'they'? And spiking? Poison? I assumed you were simply going to purchase materials from this adventurer…"

At the very least, that was what was written in the missive from the Great Church-Father. Nive however…

"Ah, yeah. Well. That's one of my aims, yes, but the most important thing is hunting vampires. I have my suspicions, wondering if that adventurer is a vampire, yeah? I did quite a bit of research, and I'm pretty sure about my hunch. So we should just be prepared in general. That's how I'd like you to think of it."

A most surprising thing to say.

"Vampires are in this town…?"

There was no better feeding ground for a monster like that. But Nive quickly shook her head, almost in a panic.

"It's nothing to get so surprised about. Happens often, see. As I said just now, they're cunning. It takes them little to no effort to simply blend in with the townsfolk on the streets. So, now that you know all that, I'm gonna have you help me with my vampire hunting, Lady Myullias. After all, the Church of Lobelia has its share of monster hunters, yeah? You people have specialized hunters, too, so you can think of this as part of your job."

The hunters she spoke of were none other than the honored Order of Inquisitor-Eradicators. They were a gathering of hunter-killers specialized in the eradication of vampires, loup garous, possessive demons, and all other manner of monster that blended into and fed off human society. I'd never once dealt with them and didn't really know what they did on a daily basis or how they conducted their missions. Nive might be more familiar with such affairs, seeing as she was able to speak of them so plainly.

Even so...a vampire? If this were indeed true, it would be quite the undertaking.

While I had my suspicions and doubts about the Church of Lobelia, I was, for all intents and purposes, still a saint. I had to do good for the common people, and I couldn't hesitate on matters such as this. It wasn't unreasonable to assist if Nive's goal was to exterminate vampires. I supposed the Great Church-Father himself had approved of Nive's activities and issued the command for me to group up with her to expedite the process.

That was why I nodded.

"I don't know exactly how much of a help I'll be, but I understand. I will be in your care."

"Be very, very careful. They have magic eyes of charm, you see. Makes anyone of the opposite sex irresistibly attracted to them with a single gaze. Even if you are a saint, there's no guarantee you'd be immune...or be able to resist. Don't depend too much on that, yeah…?" Nive said, as we stood before the venue of the negotiations—the Stheno Company's main building.

"Magic eyes of charm, you say…"

I did know of several people who possessed these magic eyes. I'd even met them.

But these eyes… Not everyone who had them was a vampire. Some humans were born with them, as well. As soon as such individuals were found, however, they were restrained and their powers sealed.

As the name suggested, such eyes were able to charm members of the opposite sex, making them fall head over heels for the user. That wasn't all they could do, of course. History has quite a few cases of such powers going much further than that. To be precise, charmed individuals were often willing to do anything for their newfound infatuation. They were unable to resist doing so.

If such an individual ended up in an organization or group, then infiltrated its inner circles, doing as they pleased… It was difficult to imagine the impact, other than the fact that it would be nothing short of catastrophic.

There was an individual who had done such a thing: Adone the Courtesan. She set her eyes at a certain king, driving him wild for her. His kingdom, in turn, fell into disarray. Many people were killed, and much wealth was accrued by the crown. In the end, the kingdom fell into ruin and was no more. To prevent another one of these incidents, anyone with these magic eyes would be immediately captured and their powers sealed.

As for the sealing…the older methods of the past were terribly inhumane. Their eyes would either be crushed in or plucked out entirely. There had been, unfortunately, no other way. As such, parents whose children had been born with such eyes often didn't report this to the authorities, and this, of course, led to no shortage of problems down the road…

Contemporary methods were much more humane, utilizing magic to seal an individual's magic eyes, possibly for eternity. This also wouldn't lead to blindness of any kind.

While people who underwent the process could occasionally become slightly short-sighted, that was about the worst that would happen. If required, the kingdom or country in question would usually provide magic items designed to assist with one's sight. As a result, most individuals born with such eyes commonly had them sealed willingly.

There were some escapees here and there, but their numbers were few. Perhaps one individual every decade or so, which couldn't be ruled out.

In other words, individuals who wielded the magic eyes of charm were exceedingly rare. Vampires, on the other hand…

"Do all vampires have magic eyes of charm?" I inquired.

"Can't say for sure. All I know is that many have them, and their gaze is often much more powerful than that of a human's. That's why they're dangerous, yeah? Be very, very careful."

With that, Nive entered through the Stheno Company's doors abruptly, and I hurriedly followed after her.

"This way."

We were escorted by a company employee and soon found ourselves in a room with Sharl Stheno, head of the Stheno Company, along with a single man who looked like an adventurer.

Sharl was one of the individuals I had to make my rounds and pay my respects to. He was a man of power in this town. The other person, however…

Honestly speaking, he was eccentric in his appearance to say the least. I looked at his face, the lower half concealed by an intricate, well-detailed mask. It was a skull of some kind, I think. It was quite unsettling. His body was draped in a flowy, pitch-black robe. The way he was standing showed no openings, and he was looking straight in our direction.

…I just remembered that I shouldn't look directly into his eyes, but it may have already been too late. If those eyes were too powerful to resist, I'd already be…

"It's fine, for now. Make sure you don't look into his eyes, yeah? If you really have to look at his face, then only look at his chin," Nive whispered, slapping me on the back as she did so.

It seemed Nive had a good understanding of how those magic eyes of charm worked. Her words were reassuring.

We moved on to the casual greetings, and after doing so, I placed a divine blessing on him. Rentt Vivie, he said? That was his name.

This was why Nive had taken me along to begin with. As my cleansing powers washed over and seeped into him, I felt a sparkle of divinity from within his body.

Was it even possible for vampires to have divinity in them? I'd heard vampires were weak to divinity, so it was impossible for a vampire to be using divinity itself. Wasn't that enough to clear him of the suspicions then? This man was most likely not a vampire.

That was what I thought, but Nive still didn't let down her guard.

Why, though…? I didn't understand.

I'd heard Nive herself was a practitioner of divinity. If that really were the case, she should have sensed the reaction just now... Even so, she continued treating Rentt as if he were a vampire, asking him numerous questions and then forcibly diagnosing him with a high-level application of divinity: Holy Fire.

On our way here, Nive had informed me she was an amateur at the applications of divinity. To think she was capable of using Holy Fire of all things... I was quite surprised. I supposed this was why she was known as a capable vampire hunter.

On another note, Nive did eventually explain herself with regards to the intense suspicions she had of Rentt. I couldn't tell from her casual and somewhat flippant attitude before, but it seemed like she had worthy explanations for her behavior. I found myself a little deflated at the realization.

Essentially, Rentt displayed quite a few suspicious mannerisms, but in the end, he stepped out of the Holy Fire unharmed. Which was to say, the man wasn't a vampire at all.

However, while Nive seemed convinced at Rentt's explanation, I felt that something was amiss. I couldn't quite put my finger on it, the reason why that was the case. If I really had to put it into words, it would just be my gut feeling.

What a silly line of thought. Rentt had already been cleared of all suspicions. Nive herself said as much, so I supposed this was enough.

After this, Nive offered a huge sum of coin as an apologetic gesture. She was quick to ride on that sentiment, however, and soon got Rentt to agree to a request he otherwise wouldn't have.

But this Rentt Vivie seemed like quite the kind and soft-hearted adventurer. He was nothing like what his appearance suggested, maintaining a cordial and affable attitude throughout the negotiations, in addition to agreeing Nive's her extra request. This really went to show that one shouldn't judge a book by its cover. On top of that, the man wasn't even a vampire.

With that, Nive and Rentt's negotiations at the Stheno Company ended, and we soon stepped out of the building.

"So, I suppose we came for nothing, huh," Nive said, sighing as she shook her head.

"Why is it that you suspected Rentt so much…?"

"Hmm… I could say many things, but in the end it comes down to gut feeling, you know? When searching for vampires, one must have a certain sense of things, you see. The gut feeling I was talking about. And my relatively rare intuition with regards to these things told me that he was a vampire. But I guess my sense has dulled, too, in reality. I've always been accurate up until now—a 100% chance of success! I guess that percentage has fallen to 99% now, huh."

Did Nive really mean what she said? I didn't really know. But what she said about sense and intuition seemed sincere. That was how I felt about it, for some reason.

For a while, I held my peace, not saying a word. Nive continued.

"Well, I guess doing the footwork is important, too, yeah? As for the incident this time…we can summarize it as Rentt not being a vampire and leave it as that. But this doesn't mean the vampire that has established itself in this town has disappeared. I'll keep looking. Will you help me out tomorrow, too, Lady Myullias?" Nive smiled faintly as she asked me.

Was I going to keep helping this person? From now on, too…? I thought my assignment would end after accompanying her to this one event…

Thinking back on the Great Church-Father's letter, I didn't recall seeing any time periods noted, nor did it limit my activities to only following Nive around. I did, however, recall seeing a certain statement at the end of the missive: "...to accommodate her needs as much as possible."

I wouldn't be able to carry out my official duties as a saint at all. I held my head at the thought. I could already feel a sense of mental exhaustion at the mere image of following this strange Gold-class adventurer around for quite a while longer...

Afterword

Thank you very much for purchasing *The Unwanted Undead Adventurer* Volume 4.

This is the author, Yu Okano.

It's been a while since the previous volume, so I was a little worried. But with the fourth volume safely published, I find myself relieved.

The manga of the series has begun as well, and chapters have already been published. I have been told that it's been well-received, and I am very glad to hear that.

When writing a novel, the story is only a series of mental scenes and images. But it has now become a book, with illustrations, and is now in the process of being fully drawn out. I really started to wonder at times if the story I wrote, if a single episode, would really translate well into a manga.

Looking at the beautiful illustrations, with a high level of finish and detail, the drawings greatly exceeded my expectations. I often find myself filled with a deep respect for illustrators and mangaka.

I never had much talent in the way of art since I was young. In fact, I was always the type who cruised by with relatively low results. I really wonder how a human being can create such intricate, detailed drawings. It's really surprising.

While it won't happen right away, or even in the next year, I would like to be able to draw one day. I would like to draw something, show it to someone, and have them go, "Ah, okay, it's something like that, I get it." At the very least, I'd like to be able to draw easily understandable pictures like that. Maybe I should practice sometime.

More importantly, however, properly writing my novels is really my calling and duty. Such days are perhaps a little far in the future.

A life with many goals is a happy life indeed, and for these past few years, I feel like I've really been living life to the fullest.

Well, then, I intend to continue writing light novels from here on out. I will give it my all, and intend to do my best. I hope you will continue enjoying my work.

If possible, I hope we will meet again in the next volume.

J-Novel Club Lineup

Latest Ebook Releases Series List

Altina the Sword Princess
Amagi Brilliant Park
Animeta!**
The Apothecary Diaries
An Archdemon's Dilemma:
　How to Love Your Elf Bride*
Are You Okay With a Slightly Older
　Girlfriend?
Arifureta: From Commonplace
　to World's Strongest
Arifureta Zero
Ascendance of a Bookworm*
Banner of the Stars
Bibliophile Princess*
Black Summoner*
The Bloodline
By the Grace of the Gods
Campfire Cooking in Another
　World with My Absurd Skill*
Can Someone Please Explain
　What's Going On?!
Chillin' in Another World with Level
　2 Super CHeat Powers
The Combat Baker and Automaton
　Waitress
Cooking with Wild Game*
Culinary Chronicles of the Court
　Flower
Dahlia in Bloom: Crafting a Fresh
　Start with Magical Tools
Deathbound Duke's Daughter
Demon Lord, Retry!*
Der Werwolf: The Annals of Veight*
Dragon Daddy Diaries: A Girl
　Grows to Greatness
Dungeon Busters
The Emperor's Lady-in-Waiting is
　Wanted as a Bride*
Endo and Kobayashi Live! The
　Latest on Tsundere Villainess
　Lieselotte
The Faraway Paladin*
Full Metal Panic!
Full Clearing Another World under
　a Goddess with Zero Believers*
Hashi no Kami: Rebuilding
　Civilization Starts With a Village
Goodbye Otherworld, See You
　Tomorrow
Great Cleric
Greatest Magicmaster's
　Retirement Plan

Girls Kingdom
Grimgar of Fantasy and Ash
Hell Mode
Her Majesty's Swarm
Holmes of Kyoto
How a Realist Hero Rebuilt the
　Kingdom*
How NOT to Summon a Demon
　Lord
I Shall Survive Using Potions!*
I'll Never Set Foot in That House
　Again!
The Ideal Sponger Life
If It's for My Daughter, I'd Even
　Defeat a Demon Lord
In Another World With My
　Smartphone
Infinite Dendrogram*
Invaders of the Rokujouma!?
Jessica Bannister
JK Haru is a Sex Worker in Another
　World
John Sinclair: Demon Hunter
A Late-Start Tamer's Laid-Back Life
Lazy Dungeon Master
A Lily Blooms in Another World
Maddrax
The Magic in this Other World is
　Too Far Behind!*
The Magician Who Rose From
　Failure
Mapping: The Trash-Tier Skill That
　Got Me Into a Top-Tier Party*
Marginal Operation**
The Master of Ragnarok & Blesser
　of Einherjar*
Min-Maxing My TRPG Build in
　Another World
Monster Tamer
My Daughter Left the Nest and
　Returned an S-Rank Adventurer
My Friend's Little Sister Has It
　In for Me!
My Instant Death Ability is So
　Overpowered, No One in This
　Other World Stands a Chance
　Against Me!*
My Next Life as a Villainess: All
　Routes Lead to Doom!
The Ordinary, the Extraordinary
　and SOAP!
Otherside Picnic

Outbreak Company
Perry Rhodan NEO
Private Tutor to the Duke's
　Daughter
Reborn to Master the Blade: From
　Hero-King to Extraordinary
　Squire ♀*
Record of Wortenia War*
Reincarnated as the Piggy Duke:
　This Time I'm Gonna Tell Her
　How I Feel!
The Reincarnated Princess Spends
　Another Day Skipping Story
　Routes
Seirei Gensouki: Spirit Chronicles*
Sexiled: My Sexist Party Leader
　Kicked Me Out, So I Teamed Up
　With a Mythical Sorceress!
She's the Cutest... But We're
　Just Friends!
The Sidekick Never Gets the Girl,
　Let Alone the Protag's Sister!
Slayers
The Sorcerer's Receptionist
Sorcerous Stabber Orphen*
Sweet Reincarnation**
The Tales of Marielle Clarac*
Tearmoon Empire
Teogonia
The Underdog of the Eight Greater
　Tribes
The Unwanted Undead
　Adventurer*
Villainess: Reloaded! Blowing
　Away Bad Ends with
　Modern Weapons*
Welcome to Japan, Ms. Elf!*
The White Cat's Revenge as
　Plotted from the Dragon King's
　Lap
A Wild Last Boss Appeared!
The World's Least Interesting
　Master Swordsman

...and more!
* Novel and Manga Editions
** Manga Only
Keep an eye out at j-novel.club
for further new title
announcements!

fifth

5

Author
Yu Okano

Illustrator
Jaian

The Unwanted Undead Adventurer

NOVEL Volume 5: On Sale April 2022

MANGA Volume 4: On Sale March 2022